**Management Preparation for
Collective Bargaining**

MANAGEMENT PREPARATION FOR COLLECTIVE BARGAINING

By

MEYER S. RYDER
University of Michigan

CHARLES M. REHMUS
University of Michigan

SANFORD COHEN
University of New Mexico

1966
DOW JONES-IRWIN, INC.
HOMEWOOD, ILLINOIS

Library of Congress Catalog Card No. 66–25592

Printed in the United States of America

Acknowledgments

This study was undertaken to fill a gap in the otherwise voluminous literature on collective bargaining. The authors are grateful to the Institute of Labor and Industrial Relations of The University of Michigan— Wayne State University for its financial support of our expenses in connection with it. We wish particularly to thank two members of the Institute staff; Doris Mc-Laughlin who edited our work and Esther Van Duzen who typed endless interview notes and transcripts, as well as several versions of the manuscript.

We also wish to record our deep and specific gratitude to a large number of individuals who were promised anonymity—the many industrial relations representatives of American business who gave many hours, even days, of their time to us. This study would have been impossible without their cooperation. They were willing to tell us of their work, their problems, and their beliefs and uncertainties about the kind of preparation for collective bargaining that they undertake. We hope the result will be of interest and value to each of them, and to students and practitioners of industrial relations generally.

M. S. R.
C. M. R.
S. C.

Table of Contents

Introduction

ALTHOUGH the subject of collective bargaining has been extensively researched—as much, perhaps, as any contemporary economic institution—relatively little has been written about management preparations for bargaining. There is, by way of contrast, a fairly large literature dealing with one aspect or another of union preparatory practices. The difference may reflect the fact that the union, in its usual role as the aggressor seeking contractual change, has provided more exciting material for the researcher, or it may be simply because prenegotiatory activities within unions have generally been more open to observation than have those in corporations. Whatever the reason, there is a surprising dearth of specific information about what management actually does to get ready for collective bargaining.

Corporate industrial relations personnel themselves do not appear to be especially knowledgeable about prevailing methods of preparation outside their own companies. Very few of those interviewed during the present study knew very much about preparation procedures in firms other than their own, and almost all were interested in knowing how others went about the task. The study was undertaken, in fact, as a result of similar expressions of interest made to the writers in the course of management training programs or in professional contacts. Although the material is being presented with the special concerns of industrial relations practitioners in mind, much of the following discussion will also be of interest to students of collective bargaining.

Method of Investigation

The main objective of this report is to describe selective aspects of management's preparation for bargaining with labor unions. The data presented were obtained for the most part from personal interviews with about 100 representatives of 40 companies and employer bargaining associations.

No effort was made to select a statistically significant sample of respondents. The results can be defended as meaningful, however, since almost all the firms involved are large-scale employers that occupy prominent positions in the American collective bargaining scene. All heavily organized industries are represented in the sample, as are all the prominent forms of bargaining structures found in the United States.

The interviewees included representatives of companies that prepare and negotiate individually, companies that prepare and negotiate jointly with others in their industry, and some that prepare jointly with others but negotiate separately. Professional management representatives and lawyers that bargain for clients were among those interviewed, as were professional management negotiators from a number of employer associations. Some of the professional negotiators are with associations organized horizontally within a single industry, while others negotiate for companies in different industries.

The interviews were conducted on an informal basis and ranged in length from several hours to several days. The interviewees, a number of whom had never before been questioned on their industrial relations practices by academic researchers, were highly cooperative and responded frankly to the questions posed. In several cases, confidential corporation records were made available to the writers. It will not be possible to indicate data sources, however, since a number of the respondents requested that they and their firms not be identified.

Initial Study Design

The initial study plan was to present the results of the interviews as a simple summary of the mechanics of bargaining preparations. It was assumed that the summary would make it possible to identify different preparation systems, and that a relationship might be found between preparation systems and such variables as the nature of the union with which the company dealt, the competitive structure of the industry, and the training and background of industrial relations executives.

The hypothesis that method of preparation might correlate with one or another of the variables cited was dropped early in the study. Preparations are affected by such factors, but the total act of getting ready for negotiations is a complex endeavor and the variations from firm to firm appear to be as significant as the similarities.

In a broad sense, methods of preparation were found to be the same among all the firms studied. Certain types of data are collected, and, on the basis of the data, decisions are made which lead to a particular stance on the firm's part in negotiations. At the same time, firms differ concerning the subject matter emphasized in preparation and the relationships among company personnel involved in the preparation.

To give appropriate emphasis to both similarities and differences, the original interest in identifying preparation systems was dropped and the study reoriented to be basically a descriptive treatment of prevailing practices in the firms sampled. Several generalizations were derived from the interview data, and they will be presented in the concluding chapter.

Content of the Study

As suggested above, a meaningful study of management preparation for bargaining must encompass a wide range of subjects. Emphasis and approach, and thus the exact nature of preparation, reflect such diverse factors as status of industrial relations personnel within the company, background experience and training of these personnel, place of the industrial relations division within the administrative hierarchy, structure of the employer bargaining unit (e.g., single plant, multiplant, employer association), and character of the union.

Often, it was found that companies prepare differently for different unions with which they negotiate. The most interesting feature in several industries is the developing practice of joint union–management participation in certain phases of preparation. The role of third-party neutrals in several situations is also noteworthy.

Various aspects of responsibility for preparation will be examined in Chapters 1 and 2. These will be followed by discussions of time elements in preparation, final preparations, and subjects of preparation. Preparation conducted by groups of employers will be discussed in a separate chapter. A final chapter will summarize the findings and present a number of conclusions.

The "New" Management Approach to Bargaining

During the interviews, management representatives were asked, "When did you begin the system of preparation which you now use?" A typical answer was that the system was begun in the mid-1950s, following some major strike or particularly burdensome contract negotiation. Often, company representatives said that a few years ago they had taken a new look at where they were going in their relationships with their unions. The system actually being considered at the time has frequently been referred to as "the new management approach to bargaining."

Recent collective bargaining literature has made a great deal of management's having more success in collective bargaining in the last five or ten years than it had in the first post-World War II decade. Many of the persons interviewed agree with this line of thought. They believe that they have been able to make better settlements in their more recent negotiations, and that wages have not been escalating so rapidly in recent years as formerly. They think that unit labor costs have been more firmly controlled, and that workable arrangements have been devised for dealing with employee security and other difficult problems. Concurrently with these developments, there have been fewer work stoppages than in the immediate postwar years.

These changes have resulted, in part, from pure market economics. Existence of surplus manufacturing capacity and a relatively high rate of unemployment made it more difficult for many unions to bargain in most of the second postwar decade as aggressively as they had in the first.

In addition to these "external" factors that have worked to the advantage of management, industrial relations personnel believe that better preparation has been an important element in their strengthened bargaining position. Industrial relations executives believe that they have come to know their work better and that they are doing a more effective job of selecting and training personnel for their departments. The industrial relations function itself is viewed as having achieved more status within the enterprise, and is now considered less a necessary evil and more a partner with other elements of the management team in sharing responsibility for and control of profits and losses.

Before the days of the "new" management approach to bargaining, management frequently subordinated industrial relations considerations to other interests of the enterprise. The coexistence of strong unions and management's reluctance to give industrial relations considerations sufficient weight resulted in many high-cost labor contract settlements during the 1940's and early 1950's. Eventual realization of these facts forced many companies to investigate and then to undertake different approaches in order to bargain more effectively with unions. This, in brief, appears to be the background to the development of the new approach to industrial relations.

Implementation of what management considered to be essential labor policy changes was easily and harmoniously achieved in some situations. In others, a considerable amount of industrial conflict was anticipated, and did occur before the new decisions and approaches could be effectuated. Whatever the cost, the new approach, according to industrial relations personnel, generally had good results from management's point of view.

The subject of bargaining preparations by management thus is more important—and more interesting—because of the aggressive stances that many firms have taken in recent negotiations with unions. It can be anticipated, consequently, that students and practitioners in the field of industrial relations will direct more attention to this area than they have in the past.

Preparation and the Bargaining Process

This volume is concerned with the way in which management prepares for bargaining with labor unions. The character of the bargaining process will obviously be important among the variables that influence the nature of management preparations.

When bargaining structures are simple, time spent in preparations and the scope of preparations will usually be less than when the structures are complicated. A small, single-plant firm that bargains with a local union, for example, will not usually prepare so thoroughly as a large, multiplant firm that negotiates with one or more large national unions. In relationships between large corporations and large national unions, bargaining preparations as well as goals and tactics will be influenced by the interactions of different interest groups within each organization.

Preparations when the labor–management relationship is hostile will be different from those in a harmonious relationship. When parties enter into bargaining with predetermined and rigidly fixed positions, preparations will be designed primarily to help the negotiator do an intelligent job at the conference table, to let the other party know the settlement point and how firmly it is held, rather than to convince the opposite party about the reasonableness of a given position. Thus, it is important to be aware of these several facets of the bargaining process in an examination of management's preparation for bargaining.

The detailed study of preparation for bargaining begins in Chapter 1. Readers who are unfamiliar with the collective bargaining process may prefer to read the brief summary of that process in the Appendix before moving to the remainder of this study.

Chapter 1

Responsibility for Preparation

MANAGEMENT PREPARATIONS for negotiations can be divided into two broad phases. During the first, various types of data are collected and analyzed. In the second, decisions are made concerning what management will try to do in the actual bargaining sessions. It should be kept in mind that this statement and most of the description that follows are based upon the practices followed by the firms involved in the study described in the Introduction. In the rich variety that characterizes American collective bargaining, a sampling of 40 cases cannot be expected to reveal the full range of what is done—and what is not done—before labor and management engage in their periodic bargaining sessions.

Responsibility for collecting and analyzing data usually rests with an industrial relations unit, although not infrequently the unit will have the cooperation of other company departments. Decisions relative to the firm's major economic goals in negotiations are ordinarily made at the top level of the organizational hierarchy. As will be noted in Chapter 2, however, such decisions are sometimes made after an involved dialogue among personnel from numerous departments.

In certain situations, such as multiemployer bargaining arrangements, the role of the expert may be a major one. Decisions on noneconomic issues, such as contract administration, are usually within the domain of the industrial relations unit, although here, too, authority and responsibility may be shared with other company units.

The focus of this chapter will be on the loci of responsibility for preparations, with emphasis on the portion that has been called the data collection phase. Our interviews indicated that the character of bargaining preparation is conditioned in significant ways by industrial relations personnel, and that these personnel, in turn, approach their work from perspectives that reflect a variety of experiences and types of education. So, we will first turn to a brief consideration of the men engaged in industrial relations work.

Industrial Relations Personnel

Many present-day industrial relations practitioners are either lawyers or persons trained specifically for personnel work. More numerous than those with legal or personnel backgrounds, however, are persons who come into industrial relations work from jobs that have limited, if any, ties to labor–management relations.

Industrial relations personnel are generally well educated. Four out of five have undergraduate college degrees, usually in business administration, liberal arts, or science and engineering. In only a small fraction of cases were their undergraduate major fields at all related to industrial relations. One out of four holds a degree beyond the bachelor level. Of those with advanced degrees, approximately half hold law degrees, and 25 percent hold graduate degrees in industrial relations.

A recent study shows that the median salary for today's industrial relations executives is $13,000.[1] Fourteen percent of the group surveyed in this study receive salaries in excess of $20,000, and 20 percent less than $10,000. Almost half receive bonuses in addition to their salaries, and one-third are eligible for stock option plans in their companies. In general, salary levels follow company size.

Most of the present industrial relations executives have been in their jobs over five years, and have achieved their present positions by promotion from within their companies. Almost one third, however, were placed in a top industrial relations job by promotion from a company position that was unrelated to industrial relations or personnel work. Of today's industrial relations men, 25 percent have been union members at some time in their lives, but less than 5 percent have ever been union officials.

Hiring Policies in Industrial Relations

Interesting though the above general statistical figures may be, they do not tell a great deal about the kinds of men being brought into the field today. In actual practice, several striking diversities exist in present management hiring policies for selecting trainees in the industrial relations field. Companies differ on the qualities they are looking for in new industrial relations men and on the kinds of training they think desirable, and there is a par-

---

[1] Industrial Relations Institute, "The Industrial Relations Executive" (New York, 1964) p. 12.

ticularly sharp difference of opinion on the value of legal training.

In the past, most industrial relations men more or less drifted into the field from a variety of backgrounds. Today, many companies specifically develop new industrial relations personnel by means of their own management training programs. In addition, when looking for trainees an increasing number of firms now tend to favor candidates who have majored in an industrial relations program or, at least, have had several courses in the area.

The qualities most frequently cited as necessary in industrial relations work were articulateness, persistence, and persuasiveness. Representatives of many companies went on to say that good industrial relations men should understand people and their motives. A spokesman for one firm that emphasized the understanding characteristic added, however, that it is not desirable for an industrial relations man to have a strong liking for people. He stated that a strong liking for people almost invariably entails a concomitant need to be liked *by* people; such a compulsion is undesirable in a man whose job necessarily entails the need to defend unpopular decisions.

Another company executive emphasized that imagination is one of the prime qualities for which his firm looks when hiring new industrial relations trainees. He indicated that a creative imagination is one of the most important attributes of a good industrial relations man. His firm attempts to find this quality by asking prospective employees in the field whether they have ever written poetry, fiction, or other imaginative works—interests which one might not normally regard as requisite qualifications for industrial relations work.

To some companies, it is important that industrial

relations men have line production experience. They reason that staff men, who will have to make their recommendations and decisions acceptable to line men, can gain an understanding of line attitudes only through actual experience. Therefore, such companies either select personnel men from among line supervisors or insist that industrial relations trainees be given some line experience during their first two or three years with the company.

However, representatives of an equally large number of companies commented that line production experience is irrelevant. They argued that the industrial relations field is sufficiently specialized and exacting so that production experience, even if desirable, is not essential. They do not feel that they ought to devote time to this purpose in their management training programs.

It is difficult to generalize about differences in company attitudes concerning the necessity of line experience. The variations appear to result solely from past experiences of management in a particular company. More specifically, it is probably related to the predilections of their present industrial relations executives—the men who hire and train their own successors.

Legal Training

Another important way in which today's management appears to be following dissimilar approaches in recruitment of new industrial relations personnel is in the use of men with legal training. Some companies are hiring only lawyers as industrial relations trainees. Their representatives stated that today's industrial relations men should have training in labor law because of the large volume of arbitration and National Labor Relations Board proceedings with which they will be involved. In these companies, it is regarded as inefficient or too expensive for the industrial relations department to call constantly on house counsel or outside counsel to advise in these matters.

Other companies are hiring men with legal training for their industrial relations staffs, not because they plan to use their legal skills, but because they are impressed by the discipline of a law school education. They believe that training in law engenders the qualities they hope to find in new industrial relations men. Representatives of companies that take this position frequently stated that they are unhappy with the training students receive in industrial relations and personnel work in American universities today. They stated that people with industrial relations training have an overidealized picture of industrial relations work and do not understand the need to accept trainee status before moving up to policy-making jobs in the field.

A third line of thought is that training in the law is a positive detriment in industrial relations work. Those with this opinion believe that legal training engenders a lack of the mental flexibility required for collective bargaining. They argued that new employees with a broad liberal arts training are more likely to have the personality and abilities necessary in the field. They believe, moreover, that liberal arts training is more likely to produce men of top executive potential. Companies that take this position usually have had unfortunate experiences with labor contracts negotiated by lawyers. They prefer to hire persons with a broad general type of training on the assumption that these men, in the course of their jobs, will pick up the necessary elements of labor law.

This brief discussion of industrial relations hiring practices merely illustrates the varied approaches that firms are taking today. The hiring decisions they are making appear to be based more upon past experiences, fortunate or unfortunate, than upon any general agreement about educational background and experience standards. It seems clear that there is no one type of personality and no one kind of training which today's practitioners feel is best for the industrial relations men of tomorrow.

Responsibility for Preparation

The ways in which American industry assigns and divides responsibility for collective bargaining preparation vary markedly. Preparation can be a unitary function assigned to people with specific research training within the organization, or preparation responsibilities can be divided among various sections and divisions of the corporation. Again, part of this responsibility may be shared with others in the industry, given to industry-wide research associations, or even delegated to outside groups. The following sections describe some of these practices and, where possible, indicate some of the reasons why companies assign responsibilities as they do.

Organization of Industrial Relations Departments

Let us first look at the ways in which large corporations organize for industrial relations purposes. A complex organizational structure obviously permits greater variety in preparation assignments and, in fact, virtually requires it.

The most common type of industrial relations organization found in the multiplant or multidivision firm consists of an industrial relations staff at corporate headquarters, with overall responsibility in the field. Under it is a subsidiary industrial relations or personnel staff at the division level, plant level, or both. The corporate level staff will vary in size with the size of the company and the functions assigned to the staff, but it is ordinarily not large; 5 to 15 men constitute the normal range.

Below this level, each division will generally have an industrial relations manager with, perhaps, a small staff as well. Each plant will usually have at least one personnel man. Division and plant industrial relations and personnel people are, in the typical case, directly responsible to their plant or divisional managers and report, in the first instance, to these line supervisors.

At the same time, division and plant people ordinarily have what is called a dotted-line relationship to the corporate industrial relations staff, at least as far as the standard table of organization goes. This means, in theory, that the corporate industrial relations department can suggest how its work is to be done and can require that certain functions be performed, but these suggestions can be overruled by the line supervisor. In actual practice, the division and plant men have a very close relationship to corporate industrial relations headquarters, and it is headquarters that usually prescribes much of their work. Divisional and plant industrial relations men, thus, have two supervisors—one from the higher industrial relations staff and the other in line management.

The organization of corporate industrial relations headquarters varies substantially from company to company, both in terms of division of responsibility and in size of staff. Some large corporations maintain a substantial industrial relations staff with full responsibility for collective bargaining, contract administration, wage and salary administration, recruitment, training and safety.

Other companies separate the responsibilities. Then, the industrial relations department is limited solely to the function of bargaining and preparation for bargaining, and contract administration.

Still other companies, even some of substantial size, maintain only a small nucleus of bargainers and administrators in the corporate industrial relations staff. These men are then required to call on other staff divisions, such as the financial departments, the control department, and the public relations department, for the background work required in bargaining preparation.

The men on corporate industrial relations staffs may have specific functions or may be assigned so that they are almost interchangeable in their job duties and responsibilities. One major American corporation maintains a 15-man industrial relations staff wherein all but the senior men are known simply as industrial relations managers. These managers may be made responsible at different times for bargaining, contract administration, arbitration, or grievance machinery.

In another major corporation of somewhat smaller size, the industrial relations staff at corporate headquarters consists of over 60 people. The staff is divided functionally among bargaining, contract administration, employee relations and communications, research and planning functions, employee benefits, and so on.

The chief variable that seems to determine whether industrial relations is treated as a single, unitary function or as a broader, more all-encompassing responsibility is whether the firm has an overwhelming majority of hourly paid employees in unions or whether it has a significant number of nonunion blue-collar employees. In firms where most blue-collar workers are organized, most of the company's wage and fringe patterns are set forth in the labor agreement. Thus, the company tends to treat labor relations as the single and primary function of its corporate industrial relations staff. In companies where this is not the case, there is an opposite tendency. Then, labor relations is treated as only one of many functions within the total field of personnel or employee relations.

In the nonunion type of company, the negotiated wage and benefit structure is a smaller part of the company's total pattern of employee compensation, and union–management relationships are only some of the many considerations involved. Preparation for bargaining, therefore, must involve many more people than the labor relations specialists alone in order that different management positions are adequately reflected in the decision-making side of the process. These factors lead inevitably to divided responsibility for preparation.

With this brief look at how organizational structure and degree of unionization affect responsibility for preparation, it is now possible to turn to other considerations that affect the assignment of this responsibility.

Industrial Relations Staff Responsibility

One of the most common ways of assigning responsibility for the collection of data and information necessary to make industrial relations decisions is to place this function within the industrial relations department at corporate headquarters. Many American companies, both large and small, assign preparation responsibility to the industrial and labor relations staffs purely on the basis of unity of function. The men responsible for negotiating and administering labor agreements simply do their own preparation, using the methods and techniques that seem best to them. They can, of course, call on the controller or the financial department to cost out certain items and to make certain data analyses.

In some corporations, particularly those of substantial size, younger men and women who are frequently industrial relations trainees are assigned to the industrial relations department, and they bear the chief responsibility for preparation under the guidance of senior negotiators and administrators. In other firms, no one set of people on the industrial relations staff has specific responsibility for research and data collection; all those in the department simply do the job as time permits.

The rationale for assigning preparation responsibility to corporate industrial relations staff is rather obvious. Those who do the bargaining know best what kinds of factual evidence they are apt to need to back up their across-the-table negotiations. They are familiar with past negotiating problems and the types of factual information that will carry weight with the union bargaining team. They are also most likely to know what the new issues in bargaining will be.

Representatives of several companies stated that the reason they keep preparation responsibility rather tightly held within the industrial relations department is that its assignment outside the department would, all too often, provide the union with advance information on what the company is thinking of doing and offering in forth-coming negotiations. Companies that make this argument state that it is almost impossible to keep secrets from the union within large corporate enterprises. Simply because of the larger number of people involved, they feel that delegation of preparation responsibility inevitably means loss of secrecy and, therefore, initiative at the bargaining tables.

Local Plant Responsibility

A few corporations rely solely on personnel and indus-trial relations staffs at the division or plant level to collect the data and information needed for bargaining. This occurs even in situations in which a small industrial relations staff from corporate headquarters is primarily responsible for negotiating the labor agreement itself.

The rationale for this approach is that proliferation of research people at the corporate level is expensive, partic-ularly when their chief function is simply to collate and put together information received from local plant people. Why not, therefore, put the preparation responsi-bility on the people who must first collect the data?

Information such as area wage rates for comparable skills, wage and fringe benefits paid by competitors, and local union and plant employee desires are types of data that can be efficiently collected by local plant people. This assignment of preparation responsibility puts the burden on these people to gather the data and to forward them to corporate negotiators at the appropriate time.

This method of primary reliance for preparation on local plant personnel is used most commonly when a com-pany has no master labor agreements but a multitude of local individual plant agreements with many different unions. In these situations, there is no great union pressure to equalize wage and fringe benefits on a corporation-wide basis. The appropriate criteria for bargaining decisions can be derived at the local level, and local plant preparation makes excellent sense.

Divisional Responsibility

Some prominent corporations are organized by major product divisions. Such a corporation may have as many as six or eight divisions, with a substantial number of plants in each. These corporations frequently put the basic responsibility for collective bargaining and bargaining preparation on an industrial relations staff maintained at the divisional level. In organizations of this type, the corporate-level industrial relations staff maintains only a coordinating responsibility for the negotiation plans and the contracts negotiated in each of the divisions.

In corporate organizations of this type, each division shares the preparation responsibility with the local plants attached to that division. A basic negotiating package, applicable to plants or groups of plants within that division, is then decided on at the divisional level. When the divisional staff has made a decision concerning what it thinks appropriate to give in negotiations, it will ordinarily forward such decision to corporate headquarters for approval.

At this point, the corporate headquarters industrial relations staff analyzes the concessions anticipated by each of the divisions and, in turn, approves or disapproves the package that each division plans to propose in negotiations. The purpose of this coordinating effort is, of course, to prevent union whipsawing among the various divisions of the company.

Divided Responsibility between Plants and Corporate Staff

Far more common than sole reliance on any one group—corporate staff, plants, or divisions—for preparation purposes is a division of responsibility among them.

When the company negotiates a master contract with one union to cover all its plants, there still is need for local plant participation in preparation, since much of the information required for intelligent bargaining must first be obtained at the local level. In such situations, the first responsibility for data collection is placed on local plant personnel. They are frequently given explicit instructions by corporate-level negotiators, specifying the kinds of information needed. Thus, information is collected on an identical basis at each local plant and then analyzed at the corporate-headquarter level.

In situations of this kind, the local plant people become data suppliers, but they are not ordinarily required to analyze or to make many recommendations on the information they send up through the corporate hierarchy. They may be asked to make recommendations for needed changes in language in the basic agreement, but these recommendations may not be followed by the company when it sets its plans for forthcoming negotiations.

Members of the industrial relations staff at corporate headquarters analyze the language change recommendations to determine whether they are of general interest to a great number of plants or of specific interest only to an individual plant. As a rule, only when a contract clause is causing problems or excessive costs at several plants will the company attempt a major modification in its previously established contract language.

When such a system is followed, it appears that local plant people still make many recommendations for changes in the master contract's language, even when they are well aware that corporate-level negotiators will probably not attempt to achieve such changes in collective bargaining. They do so simply in the belief that in time one plant's specific burden may become a general problem.

The responsibility of preparation for collective bargaining may be divided even when the local plants bear the major responsibility for negotiating their own labor agreements. When the corporation has a number of individual contracts with different locals of the same international union or several international unions, corporate-level people must keep a close watch on the wage schedules negotiated at their local plants. They must be aware of what is being done in each of their plants in order to avoid being constantly "traded upward" to the highest level of benefits negotiated at any one of the plants. In such situations, the local plant people do their own preparation and then formulate a tentative package with which they believe they can settle local negotiations. This tentative package must first be reviewed at the corporate level before it can become the basis for concessions at the local plant.

When a corporation negotiates a master company-wide agreement with one particular international union, there may still remain large numbers of individual contracts to be negotiated, covering bargaining units of small groups of employees at the local plants. These local agreements are frequently concerned exclusively with wage rates and local working conditions. The individual plants, therefore, are given the responsibility of preparing for and negotiating the local agreements. Even when wage rates and working conditions are determined almost exclusively by local conditions and practices, the fringe benefit structure in such contracts may follow the company's overall benefit policy as negotiated in its master agreement. As in the previous situation, before local negotiations can be completed the packages to be offered to the unions that negotiate on a local plant basis will ordinarily be reviewed at corporate headquarters to insure that no plant is getting too far out of line with the company's overall labor cost structure.

It is clear that the division of responsibility in bargaining preparation in all of these situations follows an obvious logic. That which is of company-wide concern must be decided on a company-wide basis, even though the local plants may provide the specific data that serve as the raw material for the company's overall decision. Those things negotiated on a local plant basis can be prepared for and negotiated locally, but before concessions are made in local negotiations, they must be reviewed at a higher level to insure that serious distortions do not occur on an interplant basis.

Divided Responsibility between Industrial Relations and Other Staff Departments

Some companies divide the responsibility for bargaining preparation between the industrial relations staff and other staff-level departments of the company. When this occurs, it is common to make the industrial relations staff responsible for analyzing grievances and contract administration problems that have arisen during the life of existing contracts and, on the basis of this analysis, for recommending changes in contract language. The basic wording of the agreement, then, is the responsibility of the industrial relations staff.

Concurrently, other staff departments of the company are involved in preparations in the economic field. Economic research units, the controller's staff, or the financial department is given the responsibility for collecting economic data relevant to collective bargaining, and for recommending to top company policy-makers what the economic posture of the company should be in coming negotiations.

Sometimes, this division of preparation responsibility is accomplished by means of a "task force" approach. Separate task forces are created, each composed of a representative of industrial relations, of finance, of production, sales, or other major divisions of the corporation. Each group has responsibility for developing management's original position in such areas as contract language, basic wages, and fringe benefits. Thus, the process of preparation and decision-making in various areas goes on simultaneously, with all significant points of view in the company represented, as corporate industrial relations policies are formulated.

Many companies that divide preparation responsibility in this way, whether through a task force approach or through division of responsibility between labor relations (for contract language) and economic departments (for the wage-fringe package), do so because they have a significant number of nonunion employees in many or all of their plants. These companies argue that they cannot allow union negotiations to set the standard of wage and fringe benefits throughout the company. They feel that allowing other company elements an equal voice in determining size of the economic package that will be granted in negotiations gives appropriate weight to total employee needs. To restate the argument, in these companies management believes that giving labor relations sole responsibility for determination of the company's basic wage and benefit structure is to give undue weight to the unionized segment of the work force in making decisions. The divided responsibility approach, they say, insures that "the union tail does not wag the corporate dog."

Chapter 2

Decision-Making Systems

THE preparation process has two basic elements. The collection and analysis of data is one. The second consists of making decisions regarding bargaining objectives and tactics.

As might be expected, our interviews revealed that decision-making systems vary considerably in detail, particularly in degree of formality. Although there is some correlation between size of firm and formality, the relationship is loose, and even within the larger organizations with relatively formal systems there are differences among company divisions. Final responsibility for decision-making is also differently placed from firm to firm. One of the most influential variables in this respect is the character of union organization and union strength.

When a large percentage of a company's blue-collar workers are members of one international union, the corporation's central executives usually play a prominent role in shaping decisions. When a company produces for different product markets and union-represented manpower in any particular product line does not dominate the others, authority for making decisions tends to rest with division management. In these circumstances, division personnel usually receive consultative advice from corporate labor relations and, not infrequently, general guidelines from the corporation's highest officers.

When joint bargaining through an employer association takes place, the larger firms ordinarily have the greatest weight in the decision-making process. In some situations, however, the association's professional negotiators have a surprising amount of influence.

Generally speaking, in situations of single-firm bargaining, the head of corporate industrial relations, together with his immediate subordinates, decides on the form and content of proposals that deal with non-economic contractual provisions. Ordinarily, such decisions are made after consultations with operating personnel whose departments or units will be affected by the proposed changes. When counterproposals are not prepared in advance, the industrial relations unit makes any further decisions necessary during the actual course of negotiations.

In some situations, amendments to planned counterproposals are cleared with operating heads who have indicated some sensitivity about a particular matter, but the basic decisional responsibility ordinarily rests with the industrial relations department. Similarly, when local supplementary agreements are negotiated or independent full local agreements are made, responsibility for decision-making on contractual language ordinarily rests with divisional or local plant industrial relations units, although clearance with corporate staff officials is sometimes required.

In the areas of wages and fringe benefits, or what is generally referred to as the economic package, others participate in making decisions. Most often, in fact, ultimate responsibility for economic decisions does not rest with labor relations personnel. Decision-making systems are more elaborate in these areas. In order to illustrate the varieties of systems found in practice, several actual cases are described below in some detail.

Case 1. Decision-Making in a Single-Plant Firm

In one of the smallest companies studied—a single-plant firm that employs about 2,000 workers—the labor relations department appears to make most, if not all, the decisions, including those of an economic nature. Three men head the labor relations department—a corporate vice-president, a director of industrial relations, and an assistant director. With the aid of several assistants, the director sees that all necessary data and information are collected for bargaining. This company does a thorough job of preparing, even though the staff is small. The three officials then make up the contract proposals, including the money package. They decide which are must provisions—those for which they would recommend that a strike be taken if necessary.

These recommendations, economic as well as contractual, are then presented to the president of the company by the industrial relations vice-president. The vice-president presents supporting arguments in behalf of the recommendations and almost always receives approval for what is proposed. The vice-president thus negotiates and bargains on proposals primarily determined by him and his two close subordinates. During the course of negotiations, the vice-president also checks with the president when he believes it advisable if necessary to deviate in a substantial way from the recommendations originally proposed in order to avoid a stalemate or a strike. Again, he ordinarily receives complete support.

The decisions on the money package seem to be based upon comparisons of wage levels and recently bargained amounts in the industry country-wide and, for skilled crafts, by wage rates in the locality. In the last several wage bargains, the company was able to hold the two unions it deals with to the percentage amounts suggested by the President's Council of Economic Advisers.

The amount of the proposed money package is treated as a confidential item between the corporate president and the three mentioned labor relations officials, and is usually not divulged to the corporate directors. This is done to avoid second-guessing and possible leaks. The decision on the money package is made before negotiations begin and after elements in the package have received a cost analysis by the comptroller's staff.

The company claims that all the fat is removed before the amount decided on is presented as a counterproposal to union economic demands. In essence, this means that the company indicates fairly early in the negotiations what it believes the size of the total package should be and then attempts to hold the actual amount to within a cent or so of the proposed package.

This company, along with several others studied, has abandoned the policy of deliberately proposing a small package while, in reality, keeping a schedule of concessions in mind to use as bargaining devices. These companies are of the opinion that if a union believes that such a policy is being followed it will never accept original and early proposals on their face, that later concessions may not be accepted for the same reason, and that unnecessary strikes may result. The company under consideration here decided to take a strike about ten years ago to establish its policy in this respect. It claims that it was successful in so doing, and that the new policy has had a beneficial impact on subsequent bargaining.

Case 2. Decision-Making in a Diversified, Multiplant Firm

One of the firms studied has many plants and produces for a number of different product markets. Each plant is a separate bargaining unit, and the employees at each are represented by local unions that bargain independently. Despite the differences between this company and the one described in Case 1, the decision-making systems are similar. In the multiplant firm, the plant managers, who sometimes are also corporate divisional vice-presidents, make the necessary important decisions with the advice of the personnel managers. Even so, the firm maintains a small corporate industrial relations staff headed by a vice-president.

An industrial relations staff official from corporate headquarters may be brought in to act as chief spokesman for some of the plants because of his special negotiatory skills. Ordinarily, he plays only a minor part in making the money decisions. Apart from doing the actual negotiating, his function consists primarily of looking for hidden costs that may result from the noneconomic provisions proposed by the union or counterproposed by local management.

If the plant manager is not the head of a product division, he will consult with the concerned divisional vice-president before deciding on the size of the economic package. Area settlements and wage rates, as well as the current profitability of the division, appear to be the main criteria in the money decision. In plants where the local union is weak, the money offer may not be much less than in other plants. However, tight management control of working practices is more strongly insisted on, and work standards are more easily maintained.

When one plant is the key producer for a division, advice from the corporate president may be sought by the divisional vice-president if difficult bargaining on money is anticipated. Generally, the corporate president, in turn, seeks the advice of the corporate vice-president in charge of industrial relations. Several conferences may be held between these officials to decide on the total amount of money that can be given. The wage or fringe form in which the money is given, however, is ordinarily decided on by the local management bargaining team. When strikes occur, plant officials seem to look favorably on the intervention of corporate labor relations officials.

Case 3. Decision-Making in a Medium-Sized Firm

A more elaborate apparatus for decision-making in connection with collective bargaining is that of a public utility which employs about 9,000 workers. About 3,500 of these belong to either an industrial union or a craft union that represents various crafts utilized by the company. Two major contracts and several minor labor agreements are made with one or the other of these unions. The minor agreements are with small departmental units established through National Labor Relations Board representation proceedings.

The overall industrial relations activities of the company are headed by a vice-president. His staff organization consists of a union relations division and an employee relations division. The employee division includes a personnel research department. The union relations division is responsible for all the bargaining preparation in the noneconomic areas. This unit sifts suggestions and collects data bearing on those provisions of the contracts. A coordinating committee, composed of heads of the union relations division and several operating department heads, then develops a final group of suggestions dealing with both desired contract changes and with matters related to anticipated union demands.

While this committee is working on contractual matters within its scope of authority, the personnel research group in the employee relations division is gathering economic data, making wage comparison studies in the industry and in the area of the state serviced by the utility, and other similar matters. This research group, through the director of the division, reports its findings to the vice-president of industrial relations. The overall report contains economic suggestions that reflect the division opinion on the size of the money package and the nature of its parts.

The vice-president serves regularly on a committee composed of the company's other vice-presidents and divisional managers under whom department heads work. This committee meets almost every week with the executive vice-president of the company, and it deals with all corporate matters that need high-echelon attention.

When collective bargaining matters are to be considered, the industrial relations vice-president and the executive officer under him, called a manager of industrial relations, meet with the committee of vice-presidents and managers. The suggestions and recommendations contained in the two reports previously presented to the industrial relations vice-president are discussed at this meeting.

The union relations officials are present, because they are responsible for doing the negotiating and are most acquainted with methods and means used in effecting agreement with the unions. They also have a good overall view of the impact of each contract provision to be considered, and have a reasonably accurate working picture of the economic and other matters to which the unions will give the greatest attention. They provide, according to a company representative, a valuable "clinical feel" in the deliberations of the committee of vice-presidents and managers.

The committee, after extended deliberations, makes the economic and major noneconomic decisions that the executive vice-president and the vice-president of industrial relations will carry to the president of the corporation. The president reviews the work of the committee and approves or modifies, but seldom rejects, what they propose.

It should be mentioned at this point that the decisions made cover general positions, economic or noneconomic, and are not what might be termed decisions on details. During negotiations, the unions and the company spend a good deal of negotiating time in discussing the problems associated with their respective proposals for contract changes. When the parties are "agreed in principle"—i.e., they have reached general agreement or understanding on each of the clauses to be revised or added—the company negotiators then prepare drafts of language that both parties will consider.

During negotiations, the company's chief negotiators may request directions from the committee of vice-presidents and managers on matters that they believe may tend to vary from the positions originally decided on. From time to time, they also report to the committee on the progress of negotiations and receive points of view and advice when the committee believes these are of value. While the amount of the economic package has, in general, been decided on earlier by the company, it listens carefully to union presentations in this area.

Before making a definite proposal, a meeting of the vice-presidents and managers committee is convened to make the final decision. This decision may differ from the original one. The decision is then reviewed by the corporate president.

Although they are reported to the committee, non-economic understandings reached in bargaining, even when somewhat different from the principles originally established, are not ordinarily given the attention that the economic provisions receive. The company relies on the skills and abilities of its negotiators in these matters, and assumes that they made the best bargain possible.

Case 4. Joint Decision-Making and Individual Bargaining

In an industry where the leading companies engage in joint preparation for negotiation of the individual master agreements with the same national industrial union, most basic and important economic and noneconomic decisions, while taken individually by each company, result from a further process of planned communication. From jointly conducted research and information collection, research leaders prepare a set of comprehensive analyses, which are forwarded to each company. The individual companies then develop specific plans to meet their own needs as they visualize them.

In the next step of preparation, the chief negotiators for the companies hold discussions with their staffs, including the official who represented the company in joint preparation and the responsible officers of their respective companies. The negotiators then meet to formulate what amounts to a common position on most contractual provisions. The understandings reached are on principles that the companies will seek to effectuate in their individual bargaining sessions. During the several months preceding negotiation, the chief negotiators meet repeatedly to complete these understandings.

Each company begins to negotiate about the same time. The negotiating teams are in daily touch with one another through direct telephone connections. Through such communications, it is possible for the teams to consult promptly with one another on all matters of joint interest. On weekends, when negotiations are usually in recess, the chief negotiators from the companies may meet to review developments and to discuss future actions. During most of the negotiating period, thus, there is continuing joint consultation among the negotiators of the companies involved.

In the late stages of negotiations when the more important bargaining issues remain to be settled, the corporate presidents, together with their chief negotiators, may meet from time to time. At the final stages of negotiations, the company presidents are prepared to, and do, meet with one another from time to time, as the need arises, to confer on the status of the negotiations. Through this communication process, continuous from the start of preparation to the final hour of negotiations, the individual company agreements have come to be highly uniform.

Case 5. *Joint Decision-Making and Joint Bargaining*

In one industry studied, several major companies prepare jointly for bargaining and negotiate jointly with one national industrial union. Agreements, when reached, are incorporated into individual master agreements for each company. It is fair to state that these companies have given up part of their sovereignty in areas in which decisions are jointly arrived at.

Internally, each company has a general system in which the official in overall charge of industrial relations (normally, a vice-president) presents to the chief corporate executive officer recommendations that he and his staff believe will best serve the corporation in the joint negotiations. These recommendations are reached after individual corporate research and industry joint research have been conducted. When individual company positions are approved by each company's chief executive officer, the vice-president, as a member of an industry labor relations policy coordinating committee, presents his company's preferences.

Within a period of several months prior to commencement of negotiations, and sometimes following off-the-record meetings between the union president and one or two chief executive officers of the larger corporations, meetings of the coordinating committee are held at frequent intervals. The industry's position on the more important contract provisions is determined during the meetings.

This industry committee usually engages in an extended discussion, and at times the debate is heavy and contentious, particularly when a proposal has varying cost implications to the participating companies. The coordinating committee members try to reach unanimity on the positions to be taken. Whenever possible, they avoid voting in order to avoid the divisiveness inherent in a win–lose procedure. Therefore, compromises among company positions are actively pursued. Through this procedure, a single industry position for each item being negotiated is reached and presented to the union.

It is the belief of industrial relations personnel within the industry that the loss of individual company sovereignty has been more than offset by the stronger bargaining position that the industry has achieved. Establishment of a benefit pattern by negotiations between the union and an individual company, which happened often in the past, no longer occurs.

Despite these efforts to achieve a united front in negotiations, no company is bound to abide by the results of the joint deliberations. Any company participating in the work of the committee can break away and make its own bargain with the union. Several have done so over the past few years. In one instance, a breakaway company negotiated several provisions that, after strong insistence by the union, were subsequently adopted by the industry committee.

The union in this industry tends to simultaneously

strike all the jointly bargaining companies. It does, however, permit individual strikes to impose the terms of the national contract on smaller companies that do not engage in the joint bargaining. There is, nevertheless, some variation in final bargains reached with the smaller firms, reflecting differences in local situations.

Case 6. Decision-Making by the Dominant Firm in Two Industries

Two of the largest corporations studied have rather complex internal structures for making ultimate bargaining decisions. Each is the most profitable firm in its industry. Each is also large enough to substantially dominate several subsidiary industries in which it operates. Thus, both are pattern-setters for their respective industries as well as for many other companies in other industries. When they make local wage bargains, they often appear to be the pattern-setters for the local area as well.

In one of these corporations, preparation begins with a corporate-wide collection of data and a costing-out of contemplated wage and fringe benefit proposals in a sample grouping of plants. The industrial relations vice-president and his heads of staff tentatively decide on the size of an offer they consider to be appropriate. They also decide how the money will be allocated and, since the company has been successful in negotiating area rather than corporation-wide rates, allowances are also made for local area wage differences. Additionally, they determine what the corporate position should be on the noneconomic proposals they anticipate the union will present.

The vice-president then forwards these decisions to a

personnel policy committee, on which he and the vice-presidents from operating and other staff divisions serve. This committee formulates recommendations, which the industrial relations vice-president presents to the corporation's executive committee.

The executive committee, together with the president of the company, then makes the decision establishing the principles that the negotiating team will follow in bargaining. The chairman of the board of directors may also participate in the deliberations of this committee. During negotiations, the industrial relations vice-president and his chief negotiator report to the executive committee, which can be quickly convened if necessary.

If crises arise at the end of the bargaining period—and despite care in preparation, they generally do—the executive committee members, including the corporate president, take up residence in the corporate headquarters building in the city where the bargaining is going on. If it is deemed necessary to call the chiefs of the negotiating team together, meetings can be convened within 10 minutes. Sometimes, a meeting of the board of directors is also called if the executive committee believes that company insistence on a particular point will result in a corporation-wide strike.

This company has been very much concerned with its personnel relations over the years, and, as a consequence, its highest-level officials regularly participate in important industrial relations decisions. Such decisions are often communicated to the other large companies in the industry, and some basic bargaining positions for the industry are discussed. No binding intercompany agreements are reached, however. The company under consideration here is opposed to joint bargaining with other firms, since it believes that this might jeopardize provisions in its contract which are regarded as instrumental for the sound management of the work force. Productivity within the organization is high, and the company believes that this is due to its having retained managerial rights that have been lost or modified in other companies.

Another large pattern-setting corporation studied collects a great deal of corporate-wide information for use in bargaining. It also gathers data from other union–management agreements made in its own major industry, in the subsidiary industries in which it manufactures, and from other industries in the country. It follows the general policy of encouraging divisional product management teams to arrive at bargaining decisions with the consultative aid of the corporate labor relations officials. In addition, each division has the services of an official, called a consultant, who communicates corporate labor relations thinking to the division manager.

At an early stage in preparation, the employee relations managers of the divisions and other labor relations officials from their subdivisions meet with the corporate staff to discuss a company-wide position on wages and other benefits. Although ultimate bargaining decisions are allegedly made at divisional levels, it appears that an attempt is made in these corporate-level meetings to arrive at some consensus on the bargaining principles to be followed in the forthcoming divisional negotiations. At these meetings, small committees, called task forces, are established for the purpose of formulating policy in given subject areas.

The company does bargain with one industrial union that covers a number of its major plants. In this relationship, the negotiating is done by officials of the corporate staff. To prepare for this bargaining, the industrial relations manager, who is the chief negotiator, the vice-president of industrial relations to whom he reports, and other executives, including the divisional consultant, visit key plants to determine for themselves what may be the necessary content of the proposals to be made to the union. In these plant visitations, local plant people are given an opportunity to state their points of view concerning the company's bargaining position.

Company officials interviewed state that the chief negotiator has the ultimate authority to make decisions during the course of bargaining, although he may clear with the vice-president. In a sense, this is true, but the negotiator appears to be finely tuned to corporate industrial relations policy, and his authority is exercised within limits imposed by the corporation's general philosophy of industrial relations.

Bargaining Associations

Representatives of five major bargaining associations were interviewed in the course of this study. The data from these interviews support the conclusion that the associations, through their professional negotiating representatives, exert strong influence over their clients' decisions concerning noneconomic contractual provisions.

The association representatives' strength in noneconomic areas lies in their having a great deal of experience and familiarity with the effectiveness of different provisions in actual practice, since they have worked out in the plants of their different clients. On the basis of this experience, they are in a position to make authoritative recommendations to the client company, and these are generally accepted. This same strong influence on contract language also appears to be true of attorneys and consultants who bargain for clients, for the same reasons.

When it comes to money package decisions, all of these negotiating professionals tend to be less authoritative or pressing in their recommendations. A bargaining association will generally give a client, or a group of jointly bargaining clients, studies of recent wage and fringe bargains in order to help them reach their own decisions in these areas. In general, while their indirect influence on economic matters may be substantial, bargaining representatives leave the ultimate decision on money matters to their clients. Preparatory practices of bargaining associations will be discussed more thoroughly in Chapter 7.

Summary

Staff industrial relations departments exercise a great deal of influence in shaping management's prebargaining decisions. This is certainly true in the noneconomic areas and, not infrequently, in the economic areas as well. Among the companies studied, no one class of corporate officers typically exercises the greatest decisional authority in bargaining preparation.

Central administrative officers within the corporation, especially the president, hold the ultimate decision-making authority, while corporate boards of directors usually play little or no role. In many cases, however, the corporate presidents exercise their authority only in a pro forma sense, since the real decisions have already been made.

In various cases, without any apparent rationale, final

decisions tend often to be made by executive committees, industrial relations committees, an industrial relations director or vice-president who has the confidence of operating executives, or by combinations of officials who have in one way or another come to exercise what is, in effect, real authority.

Professional negotiators for bargaining associations generally have considerable influence over the decisions reached by their clients in the noneconomic areas of bargaining. Professionals, however, tend to inform rather than to advise clients about economic matters.

Chapter 3

Timing of Preparation

WHEN DO preparations for a forthcoming negotiation begin? Asked this question, industrial relations executives invariably reply, "The day after the current agreement is signed." In a number of firms, this is almost the literal truth. Some organizations have adopted a system wherein operating supervisors and the industrial relations staff continuously note and file records of day-to-day plant experiences in contract administration for the purpose of building a case for the next round of negotiations.

In some multiplant firms, plant managers prepare industrial relations reports at time intervals designated by their corporate labor relations staff superiors, beginning shortly after the effective date of the current agreement. The reports are then forwarded to the corporate industrial relations staff for analysis.

One multiplant firm, in addition to receiving such reports from its many plants, has a relatively large arbitration trial staff, which in the course of trying arbitration cases around the country makes a special point of probing for information about union and contract administration problems. The information so acquired is reported and discussed with industrial relations colleagues at central staff headquarters. It is not uncommon, then, for firms to engage in a type of constant industrial relations surveillance that constitutes a form of bargaining preparation.

Apart from this aspect of preparation, however, all the interviewed companies regard the formal opening of negotiations as the date by which preparations shall have been completed. Most follow some sort of time schedule, with a specific preparation plan, that terminates as of the commencement of negotiations.

Among the firms interviewed, several begin to prepare shortly after the current agreement is consummated, while others begin anywhere from four to nine months before the opening of negotiations. In most cases, the amount of time spent in preparations correlates with the complexity of the bargaining structure. Thus, when a multiemployer group bargains with one or more labor organizations, it spends more time than does, for example, a single-plant firm that bargains with one union.

One of the more elaborate preparation procedures described by those interviewed in this study was that followed in an industry where the major firms negotiate separately but cooperate in their preparations. Each firm maintains membership in an industry research committee through the activity of a corporate research staff person who serves as a member. The committee meets at regular intervals throughout the term of the current contract. During the early months of the contract, the representatives exchange views concerning union relations in their own and other related industries. Most of these companies start negotiations at approximately the same time.

About nine months before negotiations begin, the chief negotiators of each company meet to exchange views. Discussions cover points that appear to the group to be current problems as well as the issues in labor relations that affect their companies specifically, their industry as a whole, and the American industrial scene generally. These officials meet with the research committee for full discussion of the specific negotiating areas that may require preparation in depth.

Research committee members then meet and parcel out the given subject areas for individual research. They also assign themselves certain sections of their respective national labor agreements, which though negotiated separately are similar in many respects. Thus, one representative and his staff will undertake research involving the seniority article; another, research involving the equalization of overtime clause; and so on. Each company then turns over to the particular research committee member responsible for a specific subject area all the information it may possess relating to that area.

In connection with the work done on specific contract clauses, it should be mentioned that these companies circulate among themselves all arbitration decisions that affect their companies. Each member, as noted, obtains research assistance as needed from individuals within his own company, and may turn to the industry association or even to firms in other industries. In this connection, the national association of this industry has a director and a chief economist who meet regularly with the research committee during the final nine months of most active preparation. The association provides cost and other information derived from aggregate industry statistics.

As the negotiating date approaches, the research committee members meet more frequently—first quarterly, then monthly, or even oftener. The chief negotiators of the companies attend some of these meetings to evaluate and analyze what the research appears to be producing. Out of all this comes what can be called a problem area book, which is distributed to each company.

The problem book, usually in final form several weeks before negotiations start, contains discussions of each issue researched, including pertinent advantageous contract language from each member company's agreements and, when relevant, from other contracts in the industry or even outside of the industry. The text also includes general observations by the committee, as well as cost analyses where these are pertinent. It concludes with recommendations for each area and includes suggested arguments for use in negotiations.

Ordinarily, the committee does not draft contract language proposals. In the days immediately preceding negotiations, the chief negotiators meet with the industry research committee and also among themselves to plan subject area strategy to be used when actual bargaining commences.

In the example cited above, the firms are, in a sense, preparing continuously, but, as noted, the serious phase of preparations begins about nine months before the start of negotiations. This appears to be the average preparation time for larger multiplant companies. The average for smaller firms is less.

The preparation time is even shorter—about three to four months—for employers represented in their individual bargaining by professional negotiators from an employer bargaining association. If the firm is a regular account of such an organization, its labor agreements over the years are on file with the association. One bargaining association has set up a tickler file of contract expiration dates. It notifies the individual employer about four months before the start of negotiations that the association negotiator responsible for the account is ready to confer on the approaching bargaining period. When an association bargains for a group of employers, preparation time may be somewhat longer.

Priorities

Almost without exception, managements begin their preparations with an analysis of contract administration problems. Plant managers are solicited for information about troublesome contract language, and particular attention is commonly devoted to recently negotiated clauses in the agreement. Information on the newer clauses is usually sought well in advance of other data. Industrial relations personnel are especially concerned about the administration of new items, since past experience has shown that divergence between management and union interpretation of such items is not uncommon.

When labor costs under a contract clause appear to be unusually high, measured by industry standards generally, information about experience under the clause and a detailed breakdown of costs is called for at an early stage in the preparations. This is done to allow sufficient time for an analysis of the problem and for preparation of contract amendment proposals. Those involved in preparations for negotiations frequently regard the shaping of such proposals as one of the more challenging aspects of their work, since achievement of the management objective may require that the union be persuaded to cooperate in a tightening of work standards.

When a new type of benefit is negotiated in the bargains struck in key industries such as steel, autos, or transportation, managements in other industries frequently regard a study of the new benefit as a priority item in their own preparations. Those with primary responsibility for planning the bargaining preparation feel obligated to be prepared, well in advance of their own negotiations, concerning the possible meaning and cost of such a benefit to their own industry and to their own firm.

Some of the managements studied, especially those who are lead bargainers in their own industry, make a point of having one of their researchers call on a firm that has negotiated an innovating type of benefit. Inquiry is made concerning the reason it was negotiated, its potential cost, and the modifications sought and not obtained.

If a firm patterns its bargaining commitments on those of companies in another industry that has included an innovation in its agreement, the firm is all the more prone to engage in this kind of early investigation because of the likelihood that its own union will ask for the same concession. Such lead time is necessary to make possible thorough investigation and discussion of the subject area in order that a decision concerning the firm's position can be reached if it is faced with a demand for the benefit.

It seems to be the practice, generally, to delay until much later in the preparatory period any consideration of proposals countering or offsetting arguments against union demands that have been successfully resisted in the past. Such demands usually come up repeatedly in successive negotiations, and management tends to rely on its previous preparation. If, however, it is believed that the union is about to make an all-out effort to gain the demand, a company may start to marshal its counterarguments at an earlier stage in the preparation process.

Finally, and ordinarily, one of the last things done during the preparatory period is to construct the general wage package. This delay makes it possible to consider the wage offer in the context of the total company position. For example, a company that concludes it must insist, even to the point of a strike, on a particular contract modification may conclude that some sweetening of its industry or area wage pattern may make the change more palatable to its employees. Conversely, a company with no special desire for change in its contract has less to buy and will normally fix on some pattern it favors in formulating its economic offer.

With negotiations underway, fast reanalysis and additional preparation may be required as new considerations arise. Occasionally, a new area may have to be researched quickly and policy formulated during an advanced point in the negotiations. If the experiences of the firms in this study are representative, however, intensive research and additional detailed preparation during negotiations are rarely necessary.

The one possible exception to this generalization occurs when a firm is faced with a hard demand for a benefit that it had considered to be a strike issue during the preparation period. Occasionally, the pressures of a potential work stoppage will force real consideration of what had hitherto been considered an unthinkable concession, at least by many in the management hierarchy, and last-minute preparation and analysis concerning the issue become essential. This is rare, however, since a well-prepared labor relations staff is usually knowledgeable even about benefits that it has no authority over and does not plan to grant.

Chapter 4

Final Preparation

THE last stages of preparation before actual bargaining begins ordinarily involve the management negotiating team in four principal tasks.

1. Preparation of specific proposals for changes in contract language.
2. Determination of general size of the economic package that the company anticipates offering during the negotiations.
3. Preparation of statistical displays and supportive data that the company will use during negotiations.
4. Preparation of a bargaining book for the use of company negotiators.

Three of these tasks will be considered in detail in this chapter. Preparations undertaken relative to the economic package (No. 2), as well as additional specific details regarding contract language preparation (No. 1), will also be discussed in Chapter 5. Within the management community, significant disagreements exist concerning the appropriate preparation procedure for each of the tasks. The nature of these disagreements will be noted in the following discussion of points 1, 3, and 4.

The Language Proposals

A company that has an existing collective bargaining agreement may at any given point in time desire changes in the wording of its agreement. The desire for a change may result from one or any combination of the following reasons.

First, management may want to make its contract language less ambiguous. It may feel that the current language has misled first-line management representatives, union stewards, or arbitrators. Language changes may also be desired simply to clarify or make explicit practices presently existing between the parties but never incorporated into the labor agreement. Second, changes designed to allow flexibility in methods of operation may be desired.

Third, management may want changes designed to relieve it of unusual or particularly burdensome labor costs. Fourth, changes may be desired in contract language in order to modify unfavorable or ambiguous arbitration awards, or to eliminate particularly troublesome grievances that have arisen.

Parenthetically, it should be noted that many firms may be less than enthusiastic about certain clauses in their existing contracts, but yet will not consider proposing any modifications. This usually occurs when a given agreement has been in existence for a substantial number of years. After a long period of time, most of the ambiguities in the contract either have been resolved informally or are firmly embedded and not easily dug out of the agreement. In such circumstances, management representatives ordinarily prefer to live with what they have rather than to risk a troublesome controversy with the union in order to achieve changes.

There is divergence of opinion among industrial relations managers concerning the desirability of preparing specific language change proposals in advance of negotiations as opposed to waiting for general discussions with the union on the subject before drafting precise language. Moreover, when language proposals are prepared the managers differ about whether it is good negotiating practice to submit these to the union immediately on contract reopening or at a slightly later date in negotiations.

Many management representatives believe it is bad negotiating practice to make specific written demands on the union. Some companies, in fact, do not ordinarily draft any kind of contract language in advance of negotiations. They argue that to do so tends to crystallize the positions of the parties before the issue is thoroughly explored.

It is also contended that by not putting proposals into writing, management prevents their becoming the target of a concentrated union counterattack and being misrepresented by the union. A written list of proposals, furthermore, may result in premature leaks of the details of management's position to employees or to union representatives. Unfortunate experience has led many industrial relations practitioners to believe that leaks of this kind serve only to deepen conflict potential and embitter forthcoming negotiations.

Finally, some negotiators make relatively few proposals for contract changes to the union in any event. Their reason, as they often say, is that "if a company is not prepared to take a strike in order to get something it has proposed, then it is probably wrong to make a proposal in the first place." Only rarely are managements willing to take a strike in order to achieve language changes. This is particularly true when a contract has been in existence for some period of time.

Most industrial relations men agree that making proposals for trading purposes, or proposals about which management is not extremely serious, leads the union to underestimate the seriousness of all management proposals. Thus, it becomes much more difficult for management to achieve a change peacefully when the occasional "must" change does arise.

The many management negotiators who agree with the foregoing arguments tend to make proposals for changes in contract language only as counterproposals to union requests. Such counterproposals are part of the coin of bargaining, and do not usually have the same drawbacks as opening proposals.

Despite the arguments against submitting specific written proposals to the union, it appears that most managements do follow the practice of writing up contract language proposals prior to negotiations. Companies that take this step believe that making up lists of all conceivable proposals the company may wish to advance leads to a worthwhile management reevaluation of what is already in the contract.

Some companies prepare written demands for early submission to the union in the belief that this aids the collective bargaining process and serves to channel negotiations. Having both company and union proposals in written form, it is argued, helps to define the area of discussion. Some companies also believe that when their proposals are in writing it is harder for the union to distort the company position.

Usually, the draft of proposed changes in the agreement is undertaken by the company's industrial relations department. These drafts may be checked on a routine basis with representatives of operating departments. More commonly, the industrial relations department drafts of proposed contract language changes are submitted to the legal department or to company counsel before they are approved as company positions. The obvious reason for this is that lawyers are presumed to have the ability to ascertain whether or not given language will actually be interpreted as the drafter intends.

One drawback to such legal consultation is often noted, however. Many industrial relations men complain that lawyers complicate simple matters with technical language, which frightens the union and leads it, in turn, to bring legal counsel into the negotiations in self-defense. Several firms, including some of considerable size, have had unfortunate experiences in this respect and, as a result, now place full responsibility for collective bargaining agreement language with their industrial relations departments.

Companies that do draft proposed changes in contract language in advance of negotiations often draft alternative proposals to cover the same problem area. The first proposal in a given area is what the company would ideally like to see in the contract. This proposal, of course, is the one submitted first to the union. In addition, the company may also prepare proposals embodying second and even third preferences for modifying contract language.

In a few collective bargaining relationships, a tradition

has grown up whereby each party submits lengthy lists of proposals, in both the economic and the language areas, and then horse-trades one proposal for another. Though this seems to be bad practice from a collective bargaining point of view, particularly when management would like the union to know that certain proposals are must issues, it is difficult to get away from such a practice once it has become traditional in the relationship.

Even in cases of this kind, however, management spokesmen argue against submission of frivolous or ridiculous proposals. Companies that follow the practice of making substantial numbers of proposals, therefore, are careful that all proposals make sense from the company viewpoint, even though their importance is a matter of degree. Managements that follow this approach commonly rank their proposals as must, desirable, and relatively unimportant.

Finally, when management does submit written proposals to the union these are ordinarily identified by article, section, and clause. When the change proposed is substantial in nature, the complete text of the new proposal is submitted. At other times, it is sufficient to indicate where one or a few words will be substituted for existing words. Management sometimes will simply propose that given sections or clauses be rewritten or clarified, with the final wording to be worked out during the negotiations.

Whether companies submit proposed language changes to unions early in negotiations, counterpropose to union proposals for change, or wait for mutual agreement and understanding on areas that require change to arise out of the negotiation process itself, one practice is fairly general: in the vast majority of bargaining relationships, the company prepares the first draft of the language. In some situations, companies follow the practice of making language counterproposals to the union in areas where the union has initially proposed a change. In a few situations, union representatives even rely on the company to develop language covering oral proposals the union itself has made.

Most management representatives prefer and encourage the practice of working from company drafts, since they believe that negotiating from a company draft gives them some advantage in bargaining. That the company commonly is more likely than is the union to have stenographic help and duplicating equipment available during negotiations may encourage this practice.

The practice of working from management drafts of proposals and counterproposals occasionally produces humorous results. In one bargaining relationship, prevailing practice was for management to propose all language changes to the union, including those requested by the union. On one occasion, management representatives recorded the union request verbatim, and after discussing it in caucus decided that it was acceptable. Management then made the identical proposal in writing to the union at the next meeting. The union studied the written proposal and, after deliberation, rejected it!

One collective bargaining practice, though relatively rare, should be mentioned at this point. In some negotiations, the parties simply agree on general areas of understanding at the bargaining table. These understandings are then submitted to counsel, representing each party, who undertake in further meetings to reduce their understandings to mutually acceptable language.

Finally, it is common in the majority of collective

bargaining relationships for management to prepare the draft of the new agreement that will be signed by both parties. Frequently, the company will print copies of the signed agreement for distribution to all who are involved in contract administration, and in some cases to all employees.

Documentary and Statistical Presentations

American negotiators sometimes prepare visual aids and exhibits for use in collective bargaining. Some believe that the economic presentations they want to make to the union can be done more effectively if they are supplemented by charts and other types of graphic material. Wage, productivity, and fringe benefit statistics, for example, can be summarized effectively in charts of one sort or another, and the material can be so arranged as to support the particular argument being made.

Substantial numbers of industrial relations practitioners, however, including some of those who prepare elaborate visual materials, believe that this type of preparation is a waste of time. They feel that the presentations they make are regarded by union negotiators and by many employees as self-serving. They believe, further, that almost any presentation they make to strengthen the company's case can be offset by a counterpresentation prepared by skilled union research staffs. They argue that in most cases employee and public opinion about issues under negotiation is preconditioned by general and environmental factors far more than by any documentary, graphic, or statistical presentation they might make.

Although many negotiators extensively use presentations of this kind, they admit privately that both they and the union tend to think of presentations as window dressing, and that they have no important impact on the character of the settlements. Several company negotiators claim that they use statistical presentations only as a defense against a union that originally introduced the use of such materials in bargaining.

Union negotiators apparently are also unimpressed by the usefulness of statistical displays. According to one management negotiator, the union representatives with whom he bargains always preface their presentations with whispered comments to the effect that "We'll get together privately and talk about what we are really going to have to do to make a deal as soon as this show is over."

Statistical presentations are often used in multiemployer bargaining situations to brief employers about wage and fringe developments in their industries and their areas. According to professional employer representatives, however, these employers appear to be as little interested as the unions in such presentations. One professional representative related that he stopped making materials of this type for his employer groups because the employers simply looked at them briefly, shoved the tables and charts into their briefcases, and then asked, "What do you think it will cost us to settle?"

In summary, it seems clear that while some management representatives prepare graphic and statistical presentations as collective bargaining aids, most negotiators, including some who use them, have serious reservations about their value.

Bargaining Books

Once relatively simple and brief, collective bargaining agreements have grown over the years into lengthy and detailed documents. Since hundreds of items may come up for discussion and decision during labor–management negotiations, it has become necessary for the bargainers to organize their materials in a systematic way. The ways in which data are organized vary from company to company, but ordinarily some type of bargaining book is prepared.

Most industrial relations men set up a separate file for each section or clause of their existing labor agreements. Into it, they put notes and memoranda of problems and discussions regarding the clause that have arisen throughout the life of the agreement. This file of material for each section of the agreement provides the source material for the book that management puts together for use in negotiations.

Such a book provides many advantages to the negotiator. By means of a cross reference system, he can easily pick out all the contract provisions that bear on any given subject. The materials, problems, and notes pertaining to a specific section are immediately available. This is even more important when negotiations are conducted someplace other than on company premises.

A good bargaining book makes it easier for the negotiator to cope with the disorder of bargaining. Negotiations quite often are conducted on a hit-or-miss basis, with subjects discussed inconclusively and then deferred until some later date. Through notations in the bargaining book, the negotiator is able to keep track of the progress made toward decisions on all contract items.

Management negotiators argue that a good bargaining book increases the management team's confidence, since with it management is less likely to be caught without the necessary background on any given item during negotiations. Since the bargaining book can be turned into a running summary of negotiations progress, the book facilitates the substitution of one negotiator for another when this becomes necessary.

Companies that do not use bargaining books are in the minority. Their main argument is that the books are not worth the time and effort of preparation. Some say that when a negotiator has become totally familiar with his contract over a period of years, the book is unnecessary. A few companies believe that use of bargaining books brings to the collective bargaining process a kind of formality and rigidity that is harmful to casual give-and-take during negotiations. As previously noted, however, most companies feel that the advantages of bargaining books outweigh these disadvantages.

Organization of Bargaining Books

Bargaining books may be organized in many different ways. Even the least detailed contain clause-by-clause breakdowns of the labor agreement, together with brief notations on the company's opinion of the merits or demerits of the various clauses. Beyond this, companies may supplement basic material with a history of each clause—when it was first put into the agreement, when changes took place, and why. Inclusion of this material frequently prevents, during negotiations, time-consuming discussions devoted to the date that a specific clause was added, dropped, or modified.

The more elaborate bargaining books also include past company and union proposals in regard to specific clauses. Source materials, supporting data, cost data, and other types of backup information to support the company's position are appended to the various clauses. Many negotiators follow the practice of labeling their evaluation of the seriousness of each company and union proposal. This is usually done by means of a simple code. For example, each company or union proposal might be coded in the margin of the book: *a*, strike issue; *b*, area of substantial or serious disagreement; *c*, an issue to be compromised; *d*, an unimportant item.

In addition to such materials, negotiators will usually have, either within their bargaining book or separate from it, a workbook of proposals. All company and union written proposals presented during negotiations are dated and inserted, in chronological order, into the appropriate sections. During negotiations, the proposals pertaining to each section or clause are initialed off when agreement is reached. These are eventually used for preparation of the final draft of the new labor agreement.

The contracts and negotiations of some large firms are so complex that a separate bargaining book is made up for each section of the contract. Bargaining books of this kind are quite detailed. For example, they might contain the following data for each contractual clause.

1. The history and text of the particular clause as it was negotiated in successive agreements.

2. Comparisons of the company's clause with those of other companies in the industry, together with comments on similarities and differences.

3. The company's experience with the clause, both in operation and concerning the grievances arising thereunder.

4. Legal issues pertaining to the clause, including both NLRB determinations and judicial decisions.

5. Points the company would like to have changed with regard to the clause, differentiated into minimum, maximum, and intermediate possibilities.

6. Points the union may have asked for in the past with regard to changes in the clause, the union's justification for the proposed change, and the arguments used by management to rebut the union's position.

7. Data and exhibits with regard to the clause, including cost, supporting analysis, etc.

8. Progress with regard to the clause in the current negotiation, together with drafts of various company proposals.

Some companies also include within their bargaining books prepared *outlines,* on the basis of which their negotiators may speak during the bargaining sessions. In a few cases, these outlines are written up in substantial detail. Few companies use this much detail in the preparation of bargaining books. Nonetheless, the listing suggests the degree of detail and complexity that may be involved in this type of preparation.

Chapter 5

Subjects of Preparation

SOME selectivity must necessarily be exercised in regard to subjects prepared in detail prior to negotiation, since limitations of time and staff make it impossible to thoroughly prepare for all issues that might conceivably arise during bargaining. The need for selectivity constitutes no great disadvantage, however. Progress in negotiations ordinarily hinges on the ability of labor and management to agree on a relatively small number of key issues. Since these can usually be identified well in advance of the start of bargaining, management is able to address the bulk of its preparatory activity to problem areas where the greatest difficulties in negotiations are anticipated.

In preceding chapters, distinction has been drawn between preparations for bargaining over contract administration issues and preparations concerned with economic issues. This distinction will be maintained in the discussion of subject matter preparation.

Contract Administration

In a dynamic workplace setting, the interpretations that management and labor place on contractual language probably will not always coincide over time. At any point in time, one or the other or both parties are likely to be dissatisfied with certain features of the agreement and with the way in which these aspects are being administered. In a typical negotiating experience, then, management wants to change parts of the current system of contract administration while, at the same time, defending other areas of it against changes that the union is proposing.

Preparatory activities reflect this dichotomy. Many of the industrial relations officers interviewed distinguish between substantive contractual items and administrative procedures that are construed as disadvantageous to management and those that are regarded as satisfactory to management, but which the union would like to modify. Mindful of this classification, those involved in preparation are better situated to build a case in support of an offensive bargaining strategy for the one class of items and a defensive strategy for the other.

Management's interest in modifying noneconomic sections of the labor contract reflects, in almost every case, a concern with unit labor costs of production. Very few sections of a labor–management agreement are so remote from the production process that labor costs are unaffected by the way in which the sections are being administered. In the following paragraphs, the concerns about contract administration matters most frequently mentioned by the management representatives interviewed are briefly summarized and discussed.

1. One of the most difficult management problems in contract administration arises when the contract contains clear and unambiguous provisions that hamstring managerial discretion to the extent that basic management

needs cannot be met. The language may have been agreed to by an unthinking negotiator. More commonly, changes in circumstances have produced consequences that could not have been foreseen at the time the provisions were negotiated.

Whatever their origin, the contract items amount to a language vise from which there is no escape except through negotiations. In some situations when the equity of the case is clear and employee rights are not significantly affected by a modification, the union will go along with a management request for a concession. However, when a language change would result in a definite loss of employee benefits or employee-favored work practices, experienced industrial relations officials are aware that they face a serious bargaining problem.

All the managements studied search systematically for the type of language difficulty described above. When it is present, a good deal of preparatory time is devoted to considering what might be done when negotiations take place. Usual preparatory activities include analysis of possible trading areas, drafting of proposals for language modifications, and determination of the maximum price that will be paid for a concession. When the number of language changes desired is large, or when the changes are regarded as high-priority objectives, preparation may also involve a decision concerning whether management will take a strike if necessary in order to achieve its goals.

2. Identification of ambiguous contract clauses and elimination of inconsistencies among clauses are also common management bargaining objectives. Quite often, ambiguous and inconsistent contractual provisions are by-products of the confusion that characterized the late stages of previous negotiations, when the parties were

preoccupied with wrapping up an agreement. In operation, the resulting clauses often have turned out to be prolific sources of grievances. It is difficult to clear up such situations by any device other than renegotiations. Preparation for bargaining over clauses of this type involves, essentially, a careful drafting of proposed substitute contract language.

3. Concessions granted to workers by lower levels of supervision sometimes develop into severe restrictions on managerial authority. Even though the concessions are not grounded in contractual language, they may be difficult to withdraw. This is especially true when the practices involved have become well established through usage. Occasionally, management can win relief through arbitration, but when a contest involves the validity of a long-established practice, arbitrators are more likely than not to rule in favor of the union.

Quite a few firms faced with this type of problem prepare for negotiations by grouping together all of the more serious limiting practices. This facilitates an examination of the total impact of the practices and makes it easier to choose an appropriate bargaining strategy. In some cases, the management decides to propose a general past-practice clause, requiring that all current work practices be abrogated unless renegotiated. In other firms, and more commonly, particularly troublesome practices are specifically singled out for renegotiation.

4. Loose and time-consuming procedures for effectuating substantive contractual rights of either labor or management constitute a class of problems that frequently requires special preparatory and negotiatory attention. To substantiate the case for tightening up procedures,

some of the firms devote considerable time to collecting examples that illustrate procedural abuses. One of the most controversial issues in this class is the amount of paid time to be granted to union officers so that they may perform their union duties within the plant. For obvious reasons, proposals to reduce such paid-time allowances must be particularly well prepared.

5. Several of the firms in the study follow a practice of recording experiences under contract clauses that require management consultation with a union before certain actions are taken. For various reasons, industrial relations officers in these organizations believe that it is prudent to collect and analyze union arguments for acting or not acting in a particular manner. Fear that the union will attempt to convert a management commitment to consult before action is taken into a commitment to require union acquiescence before action may be taken is usually cited as the main reason for concern with consultation clauses.

6. Standards for matters such as promotions, nonautomatic wage progressions, and regrading of modified jobs are regarded as fruitful areas for prenegotiation research. Standards that are obsolete or on which the contract is silent can produce a considerable amount of industrial relations turmoil. Many of the management personnel interviewed expressed the belief that it is possible, through careful research, to develop standards that will be beneficial to both the company and the employees.

7. From time to time, proposals for revision of the grievance and arbitration provisions of a labor agreement become serious bargaining items. All the firms studied are genuinely interested in how well their grievance pro-

cedures are working. Their greatest current concern seems to be what management regards as a large number of baseless claims.

Some firms appear to be resigned to the quantity of grievances filed and carried to arbitration. Others, however, believe that corrective action is called for when the number of grievances filed does not diminish, even though a high percentage of umpire decisions is going against the union. A company that opts in favor of a full-scale review of the grievance procedures usually undertakes a detailed analysis of the system's operation. Statistics are gathered to show the number and types of claims filed, and breakdowns are prepared to support the argument that a large volume of grievance activity has produced very little in the way of material gains for employees.

8. In recent years, employment problems associated with new production methods, new products, and plant relocations have been troublesome bargaining issues. Accordingly, preparation time devoted to these issues has increased. Changes of the types noted affect or are affected by contract clauses dealing with job assignments, special payments, work scheduling, job transfers, job bidding, and others.

When a change is anticipated, careful study of such clauses is necessary to determine whether existing contract language is compatible with the adjustments that management wants to make. Even when there is no directly relevant contract language, the entire agreement must be analyzed to determine whether limitations on managerial authority might be implied from any section of the contract.

In order to prepare effectively, it is important, of

course, for negotiators to know about the changes that are being contemplated. In several of the companies studied, industrial relations personnel learn about planned changes by making direct inquiries of officials at both corporate and plant levels. Plant labor relations people in other firms report the information to corporate industrial relations. Several organizations have instructed operating officials to keep the labor relations department constantly aware of both imminent adjustments and any changes contemplated for the future.

A number of firms reported that problems developed as a result of long-standing clauses that were disadvantageous from management's viewpoint but had never been raised as bargaining issues because they had never before been of critical importance. Given a basic change in production methods, for example, some particular undesirable but unimportant clause could turn out to be a major obstacle in the way of achieving hoped-for gains from the new methods.

Almost all the negotiators interviewed stressed the necessity of receiving information about contemplated changes as early as possible, so that they might have sufficient time to search out obstructive contract language. The frequency with which this point was mentioned suggests that clumsy systems of intracompany communications have affected the efficiency of negotiation preparations related to contemplated changes in product or production methods. In industrial relations training programs conducted by a number of employer bargaining associations, special stress has been placed on the importance of keeping negotiators informed of technological and other changes that might require a significant reshaping of the labor agreement.

Defensive Preparations Relative to Contract Administration

Preparatory activities undertaken in defense of sections of the agreement that satisfy management consist basically of efforts to anticipate the bargaining goals of the union. Close analysis of recent experience under the grievance procedure usually provides fruitful leads in this respect. Reactions of union officers to grievance dispute losses, for example, are generally regarded as accurate signals of future union bargaining demands. When a union takes a defeat hard or refers to an adverse decision as one that it cannot live with, corporate industrial relations personnel are forewarned about the direction of union bargaining policy. Many industrial relations officers, incidentally, regard frontline foremen as excellent sources for information of this nature.

Management negotiators also tend to closely watch the differences in contract administration practices among their own various plants and, when possible, the plants of competitors or other plants in their area. When the employees in different plants are represented by sister locals of the same national union, it is highly likely that the local union officers have compared contract administration experiences and are aware of any benefits that have been negotiated in some plants but not in others.

As part of the preparation process, some multiplant firms call the local plant industrial relations personnel together for meetings to discuss contract variations among their plants. Briefings about experiences under such provisions are also conducted.

Among the companies studied, the most earnest defensive preparations at present are concerned with containing union moves to share in decisional authority over such matters as the contracting out of work, shifting of production among plants, and rate-setting for new or changed jobs. Many of the negotiators stated that when drafting the language of any concession regarding a managerial right to act they are particularly careful in order to leave no doubt about what is and what is not being conceded. Several firms attempt to find language that has been tested by experience in the contracts of other firms. Some hire outside consultants in order to get an objective analysis of the character of the commitments embodied in proposed language.

Economic Issues

The character of preparations undertaken for bargaining over wage and fringe benefit items depends on the type of bargaining situation that a company faces. All firms, of course, are interested in the cost implications of a particular wage package. As a company negotiator put it: "The one absolutely essential figure that every negotiator should have in his mind is what a wage increase of 1 cent per payroll hour will cost the company in thousands of dollars a year." The extent to which preparations for wage negotiations go beyond a few rudimentary cost calculations depends on such factors as whether a firm is a pattern-setter or a pattern-follower, whether the wage structure is simple or complex, and whether the firm is a large or small employer.

Wage preparations, in short, may amount to little more than a statistical description of a company's wage structure or, at the other extreme, may involve detailed economic analysis designed to argue the company position before the public and various government bodies as well as in the negotiating chambers. The summary that follows is based on practices engaged in by a substantial number of firms, though perhaps no one firm individually pursues every form of wage preparation that will be described.

In general, the data accumulated for the purpose of preparation on economic issues can be classified in one of two ways. Internal data are those derived from the records of a firm's own wage experience; external are those collected from sources that describe the experiences of other firms.

Internal Wage Data

As noted above, negotiators are interested in having internal data that permit quick appraisal of the costs of union wage proposals or company counterproposals. Additionally, of course, companies use internally derived wage-rate and wage-cost data to counter union claims and arguments. Unions frequently do not have reliable wage information. Thus, when they make allegations during bargaining they must rely on guesses or broad generalizations from limited information. When such allegations are made, many management negotiators give union bargainers specific figures, together with details about the methods by which the figures were computed.

Internal wage data are also useful to the company for insuring (a) that proper differentials are maintained between job classes and (b) that no specific group of employees gets a disproportionate share of the total wage increases negotiated. Finally, internal wage data are used in the intracompany deliberations from which a company wage policy is derived.

Almost all firms prepare a chronological history that shows wage and fringe benefit changes over the years. The chronology serves as a convenient reference tool and facilitates comparisons with wage changes in other firms or with industry- or economy-wide averages. In addition to this wage history, most management negotiators equip themselves with internal data such as the following.

1. Current number of employees by job class, by step within job class, by seniority, and by sex.
2. Number of employees on each shift.
3. Straight-time and gross weekly earnings by job class.
4. Average hours worked.
5. Where appropriate, number of employees on incentive pay systems and amount of incentive earnings.

It should be noted that some companies make relatively little use of internally derived wage data in their negotiations. In this group are smaller firms with stable work forces, firms that follow the practice of granting across-the-board wage increases, and some firms that are firmly locked into a wage pattern that is established elsewhere.

External Wage Data

Most firms collect wage data from external sources. The following appear to be the sources most generally used.

1. Settlements negotiated in the immediate geographical area in which a company has plants.
2. Settlements negotiated by competitive firms in the industry.
3. Settlements negotiated by the union with which the company deals.
4. Settlements negotiated by large companies—the so-called pattern-setters.

5. Settlements negotiated in related industries.
6. Settlements negotiated by subsidiaries.
7. Settlements negotiated in depressed industries.

All companies expressed interest in recent settlements negotiated in the geographical areas where their plants are located. The major reason for this is that they must compete in the local labor markets for necessary skills. Additionally, some firms need this information because they negotiate with a union on the basis of area rates. Even firms that are primarily concerned with industry rather than area patterns carefully watch local wage developments. On the one hand, local movements may force them to settle above industry averages, with consequences for their competitive positions. On the other hand, industry patterns may force them above local area averages, with upsetting consequences for the local market.

Interest in industry wage changes derives, of course, from a concern about the company's competitive position. Firms also exercise surveillance over wage negotiations within the industry because the results of such negotiations are almost certain to be cited by the union during bargaining when it is to the union's advantage to cite them. A number of company negotiators stated that preparation of statistical materials that show industry wage changes makes it easier to answer a union that is exaggerating the size of other settlements. Furthermore, an accurate picture of what is happening within the industry gives a company a reasonable fix on the union's real range of expectations.

Sometimes, a company will prepare a display to show the increases it has granted over time as compared to the increases the union has negotiated with other firms. This, of course, is done only when the comparisons are favorable from the company's point of view. When they are not, it is highly likely that a similar display will be presented by the union.

Other external wage data that companies examine are contracts negotiated in the major national industries. The settlements negotiated in automobiles, steel, rubber, and by the large electrical manufacturing firms, for example, have a pervasive influence throughout the nation. These influences exist to some extent regardless of whether the company is situated in the same industry, a related industry, or an industry entirely unrelated to the national pattern-setters.

National patterns are often used as a floor for union proposals and as a ceiling under which smaller employers attempt to remain. The fringe benefits negotiated by the major pattern-setters also have a broad national influence, though not so direct, perhaps, as have wage influences. Many companies state, for example, that while in their wage adjustments they tend to follow some major national settlement, their fringe structure is considerably different than that of the majors whom they otherwise follow.

A few companies state that settlements negotiated by their suppliers or by their subsidiaries exert some influence on their own wage negotiations. This situation is rather unusual, however. A more common and related type of influence occurs in companies that bargain with one large union that represents a substantial part of their employees and with other unions that serve smaller groups of employees. The companies often find that their major settlement influences, to some degree, the character of their settlements with unions that represent the minority of their employees.

Companies that collect data on wage settlements negotiated in depressed industries indicate that they do so simply as a tactical device. They use such information as a defensive weapon against the union during negotiations.

Both parties to collective bargaining use their external wage data in a selective manner. The parties frequently differ about the external wage criteria that are appropriate for comparison purposes; the most common disagreements are over the use of area versus industry criteria. If one of the bargaining parties has consistently favored the use of a particular criterion, however, it becomes difficult for that party to shift ground in a year when the previously favored criterion operates against its interest.

In a number of the firms, the bargaining parties have agreed on the external wage criteria they will rely on during negotiations. Through such agreements, management and union have been able to remove a considerable part of the controversy that surrounds wage bargaining.

Most of the management representatives interviewed indicated that productivity data have little, if any, weight in their wage negotiations. Nevertheless, many of the firms do something by way of computing rates of productivity change. This apparently is done on the chance that productivity might come up for discussion during negotiations.

The use of productivity data in negotiations appears to have become somewhat more common since the President's Council of Economic Advisers has strongly urged that wage adjustments be linked to productivity increases. Interestingly enough, this increased use of productivity data in bargaining has occurred despite the council's "guide-posts," linking wages to *national* average productivity increases rather than to individual industry or plant increases.

Management negotiators apparently believe that it is a wise precaution to have productivity information at their disposal, although they are not always able to say specifically why they think so. The concern with productivity probably reflects not only the general influence of governmental concern but also the feeling that input–output ratios will eventually come to be more significant variables affecting the results of collective bargaining than they are at the present time.

Most firms analyze changes in the cost of living relative to changes in the company's wage movements. This is done even in firms that do not have wage escalator clauses in their contracts, since the relationship between wage movements and the cost of living index is likely to be discussed at some point during negotiations.

Fringe Benefits

Since the end of World War II, fringe benefits have proliferated to the extent that one might question the use of the word "fringe" as a descriptive term. In many firms, the costs of the fringe benefit package are more than 20 percent of total employee remuneration.

Although there is no standardized definition of fringe benefits, employers and unions have generally agreed that they include (*a*) extra pay for time worked, (*b*) pay for time not worked, and (*c*) payments for health and security benefits. Some of these types of benefits are required by law, of course, even though they are often specified or broadened in the agreement of the parties; others result solely from collective bargaining.

In addition, many employers have characterized as fringe benefits certain payments such as suggestion awards, company medical services, recreation facilities, cafeteria subsidies, and so on. Unions, however, have disagreed with the fringe label on this last group of items. They characterize the payments as normal costs of operation, even though the items may also be of benefit to employees.

Fringes commonly involved in collective bargaining include the following.

1. *Extra pay for time worked:*
    Overtime pay.
    Shift differentials.
    Premium pay for sixth or seventh days worked.
    Premium pay for Saturdays and Sundays as such.
    Pay for holidays worked.
    Call-in pay.

2. *Pay for time not worked:*
    Holidays.
    Vacations.
    Sick-leave pay.
    Military-leave pay.
    Jury-duty pay.
    Rest periods.
    Washup time.
    Supplementary unemployment benefits.
    Severance pay.
    Christmas bonuses.
    Payment for time spent on union business.

3. *Health and security benefits*:
    Pensions.
    Group life insurance.
    Hospitalization.
    Group accident and health insurance.
    Medical insurance.

Preparations for negotiations on fringe benefits are both general and specific in nature. General preparations include a tabulation of all employees, broken down by seniority status, age, sex, marital status, and number of dependents. These tabulations are used as ready references during bargaining, when it might be necessary to make a quick appraisal of the overall impact of a fringe benefit proposal.

The more specific preparation involves a costing-out of anticipated union proposals for new or improved fringe benefits. Not infrequently, an industrial relations staff will try to estimate the importance that the union attaches to the various fringe benefit proposals being made. This estimate may be based upon the kinds of fringes that have been negotiated between the union and other firms.

In their preparations, industrial relations personnel sometimes run into difficulty when they attempt to get financial data on fringe benefits experience from the company controller. For negotiating purposes, the industrial relations unit may want the actual costs of items such as "pay for time spent on union duties" or "jury-duty pay." Unless separate accounts have been set up for these expenditures, the data will not be available.

Industrial relations people state that itemization of fringe benefit costs can result in a variety of benefits to a company. Monthly reports on specific fringe benefit costs in individual plants, for example, can be used as a control device to detect unusual plant-by-plant variations.

In one example that was cited, a company discovered that over a year's time costs for jury-duty in one of its plants were almost double those of any of its other plants. On investigation, the reason revealed for this high cost was that in its particular area the plant was the only major employer that paid for jury-duty time. Judges and local courts in the area were aware of this and were, therefore, relying much too heavily on the plant as a source of jurors. The company's representatives found it necessary to go into the area and discuss the situation with the local judges in order to be relieved of this unusual burden.

Most large companies maintain current records on the present state of negotiated fringe benefits in their industry. They often prepare substantial numbers of tables that show what their leading competitors and the leading companies in the nation have granted in the way of specific fringe benefits.

Sometimes, this type of information can be misleading. It is emphasized by many negotiators that a simple listing of the fringes granted by competitors can lead the company to grant too much. A company is particularly vulnerable if complete details are not known about competitors' histories of benefit negotiations, what compensatory features its contract has that competitors' do not have, and what the competitors' total contract structures are. For example, the fact that company A has nine holidays, whereas B has only eight, might be more than offset by the fact that some of A's other fringes or administrative practices are not so liberal as those of B.

In an industry where the competing companies are quite secretive about labor costs, one firm hired a specialist in industrial espionage, at a cost of $7,000, in order to discover basic information about the fringe benefit expenditures and unit labor costs of a major competitor. The purpose of the espionage was not primarily to gain a commercial advantage, but simply to prepare intelligently for forthcoming negotiations. This effort, incidentally, was successful.

This represents an extreme case, of course. In most industries, full information on fringe benefit costs are published by an industry association or by one of the leading companies in the industry. Moreover, the Bureau of Labor Statistics of the U.S. Department of Labor publishes a substantial body of information on the dispersion of various kinds of fringes within given industries and throughout the nation. Some companies, particularly those with significant numbers of nonunion employees, keep close watch on changes in fringe structure in their industries, not only so that they may bargain intelligently but also in order to make voluntary changes in the fringe structure for their nonunion and exempt employees.

Due to the technical complexities of pension and insurance plans, preparation in these areas is usually performed by consulting actuaries. From the work of the actuaries, management learns about the cost implications of different options relative to eligibility, retirement age, vesting rights, and related matters. This information is essential to companies that will negotiate out the details of such plans. The alternative is to negotiate a fixed-dollar or cents-per-hour amount for the proposed benefit, and to leave it to specialists to work out the maximum benefits that can be purchased for the amount available.

Chapter 6

Strategic Aspects of Preparation

OUR INTERVIEWS with management representatives produced a good deal of information which, though not directly related to the mechanics of preparation for labor
negotiations, is helpful in understanding management's
overall strategic approach to bargaining preparations and
to the negotiations themselves. Information that has not
been incorporated into the discussions elsewhere is summarized in this chapter.

Anticipating Union Behavior

In the opinions of many prominent management negotiators, it is necessary for both labor and management to
have confidence in their own abilities to predict the behavior of the opposite party in a variety of circumstances.
They argue that when this confidence is lacking an
eventual healthy labor–management relationship is unlikely to develop. It is clear that company negotiators are
concerned with how well they are able to anticipate union
reactions to management bargaining positions, and they
do a number of things that, hopefully, will improve their
aptitudes in this area.

Lessons from Previous Negotiations

On the assumption that past practice will provide some key to an understanding of future behavior, industrial relations personnel in numerous firms compile a careful record of what occurred in prior negotiations. One company, for example, has prepared a detailed history, covering 34 years of bargaining experience.

The record of the past is then searched for clues to possible union behavior in a forthcoming negotiation. Proposals and counterproposals made, bargaining items accepted and those rejected, the gist of the arguments advanced, and other historical evidence are researched in the effort to detect union behavior patterns. The historical materials are also used to check the consistency of company positions over time and, during bargaining, to challenge union claims about what happened in earlier negotiations.

Alerts from Union Statements

Other sources of information about union bargaining policy include pronouncements made by union leaders, reports issued from union conferences and conventions, and items carried in the labor press. All these are studied carefully by the management negotiating team for whatever they may reveal about union bargaining objectives. Management representatives are also very alert to any hints, deliberate or inadvertent, that might be dropped by union officials during formal and informal exchanges at their plant meetings. In some cities, union and management negotiators run into each other quite frequently at civic and social functions, and conversations on such occasions sometimes produce fruitful leads.

One large corporation keeps a close watch on all items that it believes are trial balloons sent up by the top officials of a major union with which it deals. Company officials monitor all the union's radio and television shows, and do a comparative analysis of the column inches devoted to various subjects in the union publication. Finally, in several firms labor and management officials hold periodic informational meetings for the purpose of reviewing the climate of the labor–management relationship. At these meetings, a direct transfer of information about bargaining positions is not unusual.

Analysis of the Union

Most management negotiators make an effort to become familiar with the unions with which they deal. A study of the union constitution, for example, may reveal useful information about contract ratification and strike vote procedures. Some negotiators stated that they study the proceedings of union conventions. They do this not only to get advance notice of union bargaining goals but also to gain insight into the state of internal union politics.

Knowledge of what is going on within the union can be of critical importance in some bargaining situations. If a dissident group is contesting the reelection of incumbent union officers, for example, management may want to delay any major bargaining decisions until after the election is held.

One company classifies all the bargaining proposals made by the union on the basis of where they originated —from the local or from the national union leadership. The proposals are then graded in terms of the company's appraisal of the union power structure. Those emanating from one level of the union organization are regarded as relatively unimportant and not likely to lead to strike action if the company takes a strong stand against them, whereas those from another level must be taken seriously.

Another company keeps a close watch on the political situations within the local unions that represent its employees in order to be sure that it is negotiating with what it believes is the dominant group. Some years ago, the company negotiated a contract acceptable to a union bargaining committee that did not represent the union power center at that time. The settlement was rejected by the local membership, a strike resulted, and several years passed before a very difficult industrial relations situation was improved. This company, understandably, believes that a failure to be fully aware of internal union factionalism is one of the costliest mistakes that can be made in collective bargaining. The company knows now that a careful political analysis of the unions that operate among its employees is one of the most important parts of management's preparation for negotiations.

Some managements make up a book on the individual members of the union negotiating committee. These companies argue that the more known about the union negotiators, the more successful management is likely to be. Analysis of this type is regarded as particularly important when the local, rather than the international, union plays the dominant bargaining role. Companies make such analyses because they believe that the bargaining posture of local union negotiators is more frequently influenced by personal predeliction and local membership prejudice than are the positions taken by international representatives.

The contents of a book on union committee members might include information such as the union negotiator's employment experience, his vital statistics, education, job history, type of community in which he lives, community activities, and religious beliefs. One company includes data about the national origin, race, and even hobbies of each member of the union bargaining group. Such data are analyzed to determine whether the union negotiators are typical of the work force. Thus, the company may gain some impression about whether union proposals reflect the special interests of the particular union negotiators or the interests of the employees whom they represent.

The company believes that through this analysis it can derive useful clues about how hard each issue is likely to be fought for in negotiations. For example, the company once found it necessary to reappraise its view of the importance of a union proposal on vacation scheduling when it was noted that most members of the local bargaining committee were deer hunters.

Interchange of Data

At a number of points in earlier chapters much was made of the interchange of information among companies. Additional comment on the matter is warranted, perhaps, since the data uncovered in the present study suggest that the amount of interchange is greater than has been commonly supposed.

Most companies, of course, provide copies of their printed labor agreements to anyone who is interested. It is common practice for companies within an industry to exchange basic wage and fringe data, either directly or through trade association surveys. In some areas of the country, a particularly large employer serves as an information clearinghouse for other area employers, and passes along to these firms the results of its own research on wage and fringe costs.

In addition to the circulation of basic factual data, information of a more confidential nature is exchanged through the personal contacts of industrial relations personnel within given industries. It is not uncommon to find that personnel men who work for competing companies have come to know one another quite well. As a result, a considerable exchange of information occurs during their social visits or at professional meetings.

At another level, exchanges of information occur through intercompany contacts of corporate executives. In a few industries, the presidents of competing firms keep a telephone hot line open during crisis periods in negotiations.

For collective bargaining purposes, business firms can cooperate by negotiating jointly or by formally joining their forces in bargaining preparations. A very important method of cooperation, however, and one that has been little studied up to this point, is through the informal information exchanges. A surprisingly large number of the management representatives interviewed stated that their companies in one way or another participate in an informal system of informational exchange with other firms. More detailed descriptions of certain aspects of this practice are presented in Chapter 7.

Legal Standards

Both the contents and processes of collective bargaining are significantly affected by the National Labor Relations Act, the Fair Labor Standards Act, the Davis-Bacon Act, the Walsh-Healey Act, the Civil Rights Act of 1964, and state laws that deal with unemployment compensation, workmen's compensation, health and safety standards, and other matters. For contract administration, as well as for contract negotiation purposes, management must be aware of current developments in as many as a dozen areas of the law.

The employer bargaining associations studied appear to have better arrangements for surveillance over changing federal and state regulations than do most of the companies that negotiate individually. Ordinarily, an association staff member has responsibility for watching legal developments that may affect the provisions of labor agreements and industrial relations in general. Important pronouncements of the courts and administrative agencies are interpreted and reported systematically to other association staff members, and are also distributed on a regular basis to client employers. Several associations issue weekly legal bulletins to their clients.

Most of the companies studied have on their general counsel's staff one or more attorneys who are responsible for keeping the labor relations staff aware of relevant legal information. Some companies have an attorney who works directly for the labor relations department and is responsible for keeping the department up to date on legal developments. Material is also issued to plant personnel people so that they may be aware of new legal matters that affect their operations.

In preparing for bargaining, a negotiating staff will generally refer to a legal specialist any contemplated proposals that may be affected by legal standards. The role of the company attorney in preparations for negotiations has already been discussed elsewhere in this study. Regardless of how attorneys otherwise participate in the bargaining process, the role of legal counsel in negotiation preparation has grown in recent years simply as a result of the proliferation of legal regulations that affect collective bargaining and the work relationship generally.

Chapter 7

Intercompany Cooperation in Preparation

ALTHOUGH individual employer bargaining is the most prevalent arrangement in the United States, bargaining by groups of employers is not uncommon. About one third of all employees under contract are covered by agreements reached between unions and associations of employers. In addition to organizing formally for negotiatory purposes, other forms of cooperation include joint preparations for bargaining and informal exchanges of information. These methods have been noted in earlier chapters. In the present chapter, they will be examined in greater detail.

Cooperation among Companies that Sign Separate Agreements with Unions

Even companies that are strong competitors have interests in common when facing unions, and these interests are often reflected in bargaining preparations.

As noted in earlier chapters, it is common practice for companies within an industry to exchange labor agreements as well as basic wage and fringe benefit data. Not infrequently, these exchanges are informal in nature and are by-products of the close personal relationships that exist among the industrial relations executives of the various companies. Even in industries characterized by stiff competition in the product market, and where there is no formal cooperation for collective bargaining purposes, it is not unusual to find that industrial relations officers are exchanging information.

In many industries, it is obvious that the cooperation goes beyond a simple interchange of data. The major companies in the automobile industry, for example, prepare and negotiate separately with the United Automobile Workers, yet contract expiration dates are such that bargaining with the industry majors takes place almost simultaneously. It is surely no coincidence that in 1961 and in 1964 the initial offers made by the three major producers were almost identical, and that they were made on the same day. In the rubber industry, similarly, the major companies have at times made identical proposals to the union on the same day, even though negotiations were going on in different cities.

In another industry where there are two major producers, both dealing with the same unions, the chief industrial relations man for one of the companies states that the competitor does a far better job of research in collective bargaining preparations than does his own company. As a result, he relies on his personal contacts with his counterpart in the other company for a major portion of his preparatory research. Moreover, the chief negotiators for the two firms in this industry meet in person or talk by telephone each night following the close of a day's negotiation. In this way, they inform each other of what the union has said and plan future bargaining strategy.

In such situations, the closeness of the relationship between or among companies must be apparent to the unions. A question arises, therefore, concerning the reasons that companies do not bargain jointly with the union. Several answers may be suggested. One is simply that the union has never asked for joint negotiations. Again, each company may believe that the existing labor agreement provides it with some advantages that might be lost under joint bargaining. The opposite can also be true. Joint bargaining may require that a company agree to accept a feature it regards as disadvantageous in the contract of another firm.

Moreover, in many industries close intercompany dealings are approached cautiously in fear of running afoul of antitrust laws. Management may thus strongly prefer the status quo—a facade of separate bargaining that masks a reality very close to joint bargaining.

Situations of the kind described above are seldom stable. It appears that when companies enter into this type of informal joint decision-making for collective bargaining purposes they tend to move, over time, to a complete system of joint preparation.

In one industry, some of the major producers used to exchange advance information on major concessions that each had under consideration. Several years ago, one of these companies informed its competitors that it was planning to make a major fringe benefit concession to the union with which they all had bargaining relationships. The other major firms in the industry objected, arguing that the contemplated fringe was unwarranted.

As negotiations developed later that year, however, one

company originally hostile to the proposed concession suddenly offered the controversial benefit to the union and received major compensating concessions in return. The union then went to the others in the industry, including the company that had originally wanted to make the concession, and insisted that they meet the pattern. The others not only had to do so but were unable to achieve much in the way of offsetting concessions. The original proposer of the fringe concession was aggrieved by these developments and suggested that the parties move closer together in their preparations for collective bargaining in order to avoid similar experiences in the future.

As a result, the major companies in this industry now divide the burden of preparation. Different elements of their similar contracts are assigned to separate committees, made up of representatives of each company. The data and experiences of each company are then passed to an industry-wide research committee that formulates general areas of policy for the individual contracts in the industry.

In order to facilitate this process of joint preparation, the companies have made determined efforts to collect all pertinent data on a standardized basis. In this industry, then, there is now a working system for cooperation in preparations and for decision-making on collective bargaining policy; yet, each company continues to conduct independent negotiations with the union.

Although it is fairly common for the joint decision-making to take place at the industrial relations staff level, cooperation on decisions may also be achieved at higher levels of management hierarchies. In several industries, the chief executives of the major companies meet, either formally or informally, to discuss general areas of understanding concerning the directions in which they plan to go during negotiations.

In some situations, these exchanges are quite informal and take place at social clubs to which all belong. This social type of meeting occurs most frequently among presidents of noncompeting companies in a given geographical area.

In one area, the president of a large corporation invites the presidents from other large companies of the region to regular quarterly meetings. At these sessions, the various presidents discuss developments in labor–management relations within their particular industries. They discuss the bargaining climate, and each speculates on what this may mean in terms of his own firm's actions in forthcoming negotiations. The discussants attempt to reach a general agreement on the size of the economic package that each will grant in negotiations.

At one time in the past, this group attempted to get binding agreements concerning what they would or would not do in their individual negotiations. This did not prove to be satisfactory, however. One participating company head had agreed that he would not settle above a given total cost, but later, during the course of his negotiations, he was forced to exceed this figure in order to avoid a work stoppage. In embarrassment, he refused to participate in any further meetings.

As a result of this experience, the company presidents now simply agree on general areas and general ranges within which they will negotiate. They agree, in addition, to notify the other members of the group before they exceed the areas of common agreement.

In some industries, a similar, but even closer, type of

relationship exists between the presidents of competing companies. For example, during the last week of their simultaneous but separate negotiations, all the company presidents in one industry come together at one location. Each maintains liaison with his individual chief negotiator.

When one company is faced with a final union proposal, the negotiator so informs his company president. That president is then able to immediately convene the heads of all the other companies, and the group can discuss each company's further action. Each president then communicates the sense of the discussions to his respective negotiator. Here again, the formal condition of individual negotiations, in fact, closely approximates joint bargaining.

Joint Preparation in the Basic Steel Industry

The system of joint preparation and joint bargaining that has evolved in the basic steel industry is worthy of special note. It has been extensively discussed elsewhere[1] as it reflects a contemporary highlight in the development of cooperative preparation systems among companies.

The development of industry-wide negotiations among the major producers in the basic steel industry has been a gradual process. Individual preparation and negotiations among unionized steel firms was the rule prior to World War II. During World War II, the necessity of making joint presentations before the War Labor Board encouraged the basic steel companies to unite so that they might cooperate in certain phases of the presentations.

---

[1] For example, R. Heath Larry, "Steel's Human Relations Committee," *Steelways*, September, 1963.

Following World War II, a number of these same companies cooperated in the establishment of a joint union–management job evaluation program in the industry. The negotiations that resulted from this effort to rationalize the steel wage structure—negotiations that took place over a period of years—tended to further draw the companies together. In addition, during all these years the United Steelworkers of America had been pressing for industry-wide negotiations.

As a result of these developments and pressures, the companies began to join for collective bargaining purposes. Initially, they followed a typical pattern of joint consultation during their separate negotiations. U.S. Steel led in negotiations at first, but in later years decisions were made on the basis of consultations among the major producers. Finally, during the late 1950's, the industry moved to joint negotiations with the steelworkers, at least as far as the basic economic package was concerned.

However, each company then, as now, still signed its own contract with the union. These contracts were, and are, similar in broad outline, but they vary in specific details. For example, the negotiated industry-wide bargain leaves some areas, such as the size of labor pools, to individual plant or company bargaining. Another area negotiated individually is the type of incentive payment plan each company maintains in its plants. However, only those matters specifically delegated in the master contract to individual companies and local unions can be negotiated at the plant or company level.

Preparation for collective bargaining in the basic steel industry today is a continuous process that takes place at three levels. Thus, preparation is divided among the

Industry Research Committee, the Industry Coordinating Committee, and the Human Relations Committee.

The Research Committee is composed of representatives from each of the basic steel companies associated for collective bargaining purposes. The specific tasks or assignments of the Research Committee are provided by the Industry Coordinating Committee.

Individual research projects—a study of pattern-following by steel fabricators, for example—are then assigned to separate subcommittees of the Research Committee. A large project might even be broken down into a number of subcommittees, each headed by a representative of a different steel company. The Research Committee has the additional functions of watching settlements made in other industries and of collecting all statistical data needed by the negotiators in basic steel.

In addition to these general assignments, the Research Committee may be given special projects involving particularly difficult industrial relations problems that arise in plants of any individual company. A company encumbered with such a problem alerts the Industry Coordinating Committee, which then directs the Research Committee to investigate the company's trouble and to find out whether it exists within plants of other companies. If solutions for common problems are derived as a result of this activity, they are exchanged throughout the industry. Where no administrative solution is available, it becomes a matter for future negotiations.

The fundamental purpose of all the effort described above is to prepare studies and data for submission to the Industry Coordinating Committee. This basic decision-making committee for the industry is composed of one representative from each company.

The Industry Coordinating Committee is responsible for hammering out a mutual agreement among the companies on the position the industry will take in negotiations with the steelworkers union. The Industry Coordinating Committee's final recommendations must, of course, go to the chief executives of each steel company, who make the final decision. In most cases, however, the decision is to ratify the results achieved by the Industry Coordinating Committee.

It should be noted that the cooperative approach among the companies applies only to the negotiations with the United Steelworkers of America. When companies in the basic steel industry negotiate with other unions, as they all do, they engage in their own preparation and negotiation. In these situations, they often consult with other affected companies, but they are not bound to a collective decision.

Within the Industry Coordinating Committee, the industry's position is determined through a discussion process. Each company has equal weight and equal voice in the decision. Those companies that will be affected most adversely by a given steelworkers union proposal argue as strongly as they can for their positions. Ordinarily, problems of this kind can be resolved through mutual accommodation.

When, as occasionally happens, such accommodation is not possible, the matter is resolved by vote. A majority vote determines the industry's position; the result is that occasionally a particular company may have to accede to a position that is not agreeable and that it may consider harmful to its individual interests. The alternative is withdrawal from the industry group, an option that is available but has not often been exercised.

The effect of this decision-making system is that each company has given up a part of its individual sovereignty. Participating companies no longer have complete freedom to determine their individual positions in collective bargaining. The explanation for their willingness to sacrifice their right of totally independent judgment appears to be simply that the companies believe that the loss of freedom involved is more than offset by the fact that as a united industry they are much stronger vis-à-vis the United Steelworkers of America.

The Human Relations Committee played only a small role in the 1965 negotiations. The work of this committee is explained in the next chapter.

Industry Associations

Many industries have well-established associations. Most of these are primarily engaged in public relations or lobbying work, although a few conduct some kinds of basic industry research. In addition to these functions, many associations have also assumed responsibility for conducting an exchange of industrial relations information among member companies. In the steel industry, for example, the American Iron and Steel Institute receives wage, fringe, and labor cost data from all institute members. The AISI merges the data into general industry statistics, which are released throughout the industry and to the general public as well.

The Edison Institute in Chicago receives individual company data and provides industry figures to electric utilities throughout the United States. Similarly, in the rubber industry, the railroad industry, and many others the industry association has become a clearinghouse for industry wage and fringe data. When the relationship between companies in an industry is not close, the association provides a means whereby general information may be made available to all without revealing the identities of individual firms. In situations of this type, each company submits various types of data to the association, which derives industry-wide aggregate figures and averages.

A variation of this procedure occurs when the industry association sets up tables that list each company's costs and negotiated contract rates separately but hide the identity of the individual company. Such tabulated information, for example, may show that company A's costs for washup time are 1 cent per payroll hour; company B's costs for the same fringe are 3 cents per payroll hour, and so on. Each company is made aware of only its own designation.

This kind of tabulation makes it possible for each company to check its labor costs against those of other firms. If more specific information is desired, any company can say to the association, "We, company A, would like to exchange information directly with the company whose code designation is F." If company F is agreeable, the association identifies the two companies to each other.

In one industry, certain labor costs are considered trade secrets, and the individual companies refuse to submit such information to their association, even in confidence. The companies, nevertheless, want to know where they stand relative to the industry average for these costs. To obtain this information, the companies submit their statistics to a private accounting firm that specializes in handling confidential materials. The accounting firm then computes an industry average that is released to all.

Secrecy to this degree, once commonplace in American

industry, has become rather rare. Many companies that compete vigorously for their share of the sales market have given up competing with one another on the basis of labor costs. Thus, they are quite willing to provide labor cost information to competitors as long as the arrangement is reciprocal.

The work of one other type of industry association should be noted at this point. In several parts of the country, associations have been created specifically to serve employers generally as data-gathering and research organizations. These associations serve all industries in a given geographical area rather than a specific industry.

The Federated Employers of San Francisco is an example of this type of association. The San Francisco association maintains a permanent staff of approximately 12 full-time researchers who are engaged in the analysis of labor contracts, wage rates, fringe benefits, and other matters. Information on these subjects is made available to any company or bargaining association that is a member.

Employer service associations also prepare bargaining books, statistical presentations, and arbitration briefs on commission from member companies. This type of research association should not be confused with the employer bargaining associations to be discussed next.

Employer Associations

The multiemployer form of bargaining has existed for decades in some industries and in some areas of the country. Its persistence and continuing growth suggest that recognizable advantages accrue to both large and small employers from the associational approach to dealing with unions. The following paragraphs summarize these advantages.

1. As a member of an association, each employer can play a part in determining the labor conditions prevalent in his community or industry. Association agreements frequently establish industry or area patterns. Small employers often have little bargaining power unless they are members of a multiemployer bargaining association.

2. Association bargaining maintains a similarity of labor conditions among employers. Many employers regard this as advantageous for themselves as well as for the unions. In areas where multiemployer bargaining in a particular industry is prevalent, a new employer is very frequently forced by the union to meet the association pattern. Thus, the new employer might just as well join the association and have some voice in setting the pattern, since he will have to meet it in any event.

3. Association bargaining prevents union use of the whipsaw tactic. When a number of employers in the same industry negotiate independently, a union is often able to force several firms into a continuous escalation of wages and working conditions by forcing each employer to improve slightly on the conditions negotiated with another. By subscribing to the association master contract approach, a company can be assured that a single agreement determines the price of labor in the industry for the duration of the contract.

4. Through use of the association device, employers can pool their financial resources to hire the best available outside talent to prepare for bargaining and to guide their negotiations. Small companies often find it impossible to maintain a competent industrial relations staff, and outside consultants' fees can often be more than a

small employer can afford to pay. Through a pooling of resources, a group of companies can be served by expert negotiators. Moreover, the industrial relations people retained by the association can provide services to association members during the life of their union contracts. Grievance administration, help in preparing and presenting arbitration cases, and administration of complicated fringe programs are examples.

5. Through the association, individual employers can be better informed of industrial relations developments that affect their firms. Some firms may find it difficult to keep abreast of important collective bargaining developments. The sharing of experiences and information occurs almost as a matter of course among association members.

The advantages that accrue from membership in an association have some offsetting disadvantages. The most obvious disadvantage is that an employer who becomes a member of the association loses his freedom to settle with the union on terms he may be able to get through individual bargaining. Whatever system of decision-making is used in an association, it is always possible that a particular employer may have to go along with something that he may not want to do or may not have done if he were acting alone. Moreover, it is always possible that he may be struck, or asked to lock out his employees, because of group interests that he does not share.

Another drawback of multiemployer bargaining is that a company may have to increase its labor costs as a price of membership. In dealing with any association, the union tends to force upgrading of the master contract language or benefits toward the language or benefits the union considers most favorable to it in an employer's previous contract. Thus, some employers may find themselves pushed toward the benefits given by companies best able to pay or least able to resist union pressure. In practice, this drawback is not ordinarily a serious one, because it is unusual for any individual company to have contract language or terms substantially better than its competitors.

Employer Association Representatives

Employer associations are of two types. The most common is the horizontal association. Here, firms in a given industry associate to negotiate a master agreement that covers all or most employers in the industry who do business in a city, local area, or even a region. Such an association of employers usually hires a full-time professional industrial relations man—a person who ordinarily will have had prior experience as an employer or an industrial relations executive within the particular industry. A less common type of employer association is the vertical association, in which industrial relations practitioners represent, for collective bargaining purposes, single companies or groups of companies in different industries in a particular geographical area.

The professional staffs of employer associations vary widely in size. A one- or two-man staff is characteristic of horizontal associations, whereas the staffs of vertical associations are often quite large. One western association of the vertical type maintains a managing director, six professional negotiators, two lawyers, one man with specific responsibility for aiding the personnel work of nonunion employer members, and one full-time research person. Another vertical association has a staff that consists of a director, eight negotiators, three full-time research workers, and three people who devote their time to training and personnel work for member firms.

The employer association negotiators interviewed for this study appeared to be anxious to disclaim any anti-union bias in their approaches. As one negotiator put it, "While we are pro-business in our orientation, we are not anti-union." Another stated, "We are all through fighting unions in our part of the country." In general, these professional management representatives feel that while they need a reputation for toughness, they also need the respect of union leaders.

In several cases, individual companies have been asked to resign from employer associations because the association leaders felt that the particular member was guilty of bad faith in dealing with his union. These associations will, of course, represent or help a firm that has not been unionized, and may even guide such a firm in personnel practices designed to maintain a satisfied work force and thus discourage unionization. Most associations, however, will not represent or guide an employer whose purpose is to drive a local union from his plant.

The backgrounds of association industrial relations men are varied. Many have been on the industrial relations staff of a company that is an association member. Some have legal training, but this is the exception rather than the rule. Employer association representatives state that it is difficult to keep a good lawyer interested in the association and out of his own practice. Some argue that hiring a lawyer is dangerous because, "Before you know it, he is in private practice with two or three of your association members as his first clients."

The employer associations complain of difficulty in

finding new staff negotiators who meet their specifications. They believe that their men must be extremely flexible in order to cope with the variety of problems that arise in negotiations for different employers with different unions. Experience has shown them that industrial relations men whose experience has been with a single firm are often too wedded to that firm's way of doing things and, thus, they lack the flexibility that employer association work requires. Consequently, many associations hire relatively inexperienced men for their staffs in an attempt to train their own negotiators.

The larger associations maintain research staffs to aid their negotiators. These research departments fulfill for association members many of the functions performed by the industrial relations staffs of large corporations.

The research director for one of the larger associations believes that his department's biggest contribution to the association's program has been to make employers aware of the need for sharing relevant information. Before his association and its research department were established, most employers in the area tended to be highly secretive about labor cost data. In recent years, however, the same employers have come to realize that they have a common interest in maximizing the amount of information that is available to all.

Almost without exception, professional industrial relations men who represent associations emphasize that one important function they perform is the maintenance of a close relationship with the unions. They must be in continuous contact with union representatives, must know where the unions are going, and must know where the potential industrial relations trouble spots are located. As a result of these day-to-day relationships with union representatives, they believe that they are able to evaluate which union positions are real and which are merely window dressing.

In general, the association representatives think they do a better job of maintaining relationships with union representatives than do the full-time industrial relations men who work for large corporations. An association man believes that if he is doing his job properly the union representatives with whom he deals view him as a kind of middleman between the union and the employer.

While professional representatives are, of course, primarily concerned with the employers' interests, the unions know that association men will, nonetheless, assume the responsibility for telling employer members when they are off base in their dealings with employees and in their administration of the union contract.

Several of the larger employer associations place considerable emphasis on training personnel men in their member companies. They hope, through the training device, to achieve a number of goals. They seek, for example, to convince individual company representatives of the importance of advising the professional negotiators of anticipated problems, new products, or new methods that their employer members might undertake.

In their training activities, the associations also place considerable stress on the proper way to handle individual employee disciplinary actions. Many association spokesmen are quite proud of the fact that as a result of association training programs most of their employers have established specific procedures for handling disciplinary actions. Association representatives state that employers whom they represent will no longer discharge an employee without first consulting with the association.

Through bitter experience, employers have learned that hasty or arbitrary discharges will not be upheld in arbitration. If the association representatives believe that the employer has not made a record that justifies the discharge, they will oppose the discharge action, thereby, they believe, saving their member firm from needless hostility and expense.

Bargaining in Multiemployer Groups

Employer groups associated for bargaining purposes range in size from the very small to the very large. In some areas of the United States, two or three small companies that employ, all told, no more than several hundred people have associated to negotiate a city-wide contract in their industry. On the West Coast, bargaining associations are operative in such small-scale industries as casket manufacturing, upholstered outdoor furniture, custom draperies, and lace curtain manufacturing.

Somewhat larger associations exist on an area-wide basis. The brewers commonly unite for collective bargaining purposes; in many parts of the country, the producers of potato chips and pretzels have an association as well. Still larger associations that negotiate a master contract covering all employer members in a given area are found in the pulp and paper industry and in various kinds of metal fabrication.

The single master agreement negotiated by some of these large associations covers hundreds of firms that employ tens of thousands of workers. Preparing for negotiations when such large numbers of employers are involved can be a complex affair, since different members of the association have diverse as well as similar problems and interests.

During the lifetime of an existing contract, professional staff members of an association maintain communications with key employers regarding developments in their industry, and they carefully watch key settlements that will affect forthcoming negotiations in one way or another. Associations commonly put out a weekly or monthly newsletter, which describes, among other things, key settlements that have some kind of pattern impact on the industry.

By these means, employer members begin to be conditioned to a general range of the settlements that are occurring in similar industries in other parts of the country. Thus, by the time their own contract is open for renegotiation, the employer members have a fairly clear idea of the size of the economic package their association will have to grant. Parenthetically, it should be noted that the representatives of many unions are not averse to telling individual employers what they expect to get, thus further preconditioning employer thinking.

Several months before the reopening date of an association's master contract, the association staff may seek power of attorney from each employer member. This power normally binds the members to remain in the association during the forthcoming negotiations and to accept the resulting contract settlement.

Variations exist in the time during which such power of attorney is binding. In one group, for example, the agreement stipulates that a member firm may withdraw from the association at any time prior to the point when the first offer to the union is made. If a firm is in the association at the time of this first offer, however, it must remain in during the entire negotiation and it is bound by the terms of the settlement. Ordinarily, the powers of attorney obtained for collective bargaining purposes expire at the time a given negotiation is completed and the contract is signed.

As soon as the group knows clearly which firms will join together in bargaining with the union, the professional staff of the association asks that the members select from among themselves employer representatives that will constitute a policy committee. The professional negotiators will be guided by this committee during the bargaining period.

Selection of the employer committee is, theoretically, a democratic decision made by all members of the association. In practice, this decision is usually made by the professional staff of the association, which selects members that, in its opinion, will make a representative group of employers. Again, in practice, these policy committees tend to have the same members over a period of years. The result is that a particular group of employer representatives becomes experienced in negotiations and ordinarily has the confidence of other firms in the association.

In groups made up of large numbers of employers, the association staff may send a detailed questionnaire to all member companies. The questionnaire covers such subjects as numbers of employees in various classifications, their rates per hour, total employment and anticipated employment, and a forecast of future business conditions. The questionnaire may also ask the firms to identify troublesome sections of the existing agreement. The completed questionnaires are then analyzed by the association staff and become the base for discussions between the staff and the employer policy committee.

One of the first subjects discussed in employer policy committee meetings is the general economic condition of the industry. The committee and the association staff then take up problems that have arisen during the life of the preceding agreement. The staff will frequently recommend specific language changes in the old agreement. Based on these discussions, the professional staff prepares drafts of proposals for contract language changes.

A difficult aspect of association bargaining, particularly when the association serves a large number of employers, is that contract language in master agreements often must be somewhat vague and unspecific because of the wide variations in shop practices among the employer members. Until the time when all the employers can agree on common shop practices, the master contract language must be general—a kind of tent under which all the employer practices can be accommodated.

It is not usual in most associations for members of the employer policy committee to discuss in any detail the economic package that they will offer in the forthcoming negotiations. Ordinarily, the committee wants to have details of the union demands before it talks about its offer.

Furthermore, the association staff usually discourages early discussion of a money offer, since the content of such discussions has a way of leaking out to the union, and the highest figure that any employer member of the group is willing to consider inevitably becomes a floor for the union's demand. As one association representative put it, "It's pretty discouraging to have the union spokesman come into the meeting room and say, 'that offer you are going to make us today is unacceptable.' "

The role of the professional staff negotiator during

bargaining appears to be similar in most associations. Almost invariably, in bargaining sessions the professional staff member is the spokesman for the entire employer group. Staff members also participate in employer caucuses and meetings.

Most association negotiators state that while they do not hesitate to suggest changes in contract language to their employer members, they do not attempt to play a prominent role in determination of the size of the economic package that will be offered to the union. They believe, particularly in associations composed of large and strong firms, that the professional's role relative to the economic package should be that of fact-gatherer and data-analyzer, but that he should not attempt to spend the employers' money.

When differences of opinion exist within the employer group concerning the amount of money that should be placed in the economic package, the professional staff members may attempt to mediate the intra-association dispute. The staff members believe they can mediate more effectively if they have not associated themselves with any specific position relative to the economic package.

Practices vary in regard to the economic package, of course. In associations composed entirely of small employers, the professional staff representatives may play a leading role in decision-making throughout the process of negotiations. When a professional negotiator is bargaining for a single firm, he may have to tell the employer the specific pattern situation he faces and the amount he must pay in order to avoid a work stoppage.

There are even some multiemployer groups in which the professional staff negotiates a contract without the participation of an employer policy committee or without employer members on the negotiating committee. In these situations, the member firms have full confidence in their association representatives and accept any contract that can be negotiated for them. Staff members in a few instances have made off-the-record deals with the union, conditional on their being able to sell them to the employers. There are, of course, obvious dangers to this approach.

When the staff in an association does not play a prominent role in making the decision about the money offer, differences among employer members are resolved in various ways. The most popular is the so-called Quaker Meeting—a thorough discussion, resulting in final agreement among all the employers on the policy and negotiating committees.

When agreement through discussion is not possible, a decision is usually reached by means of a voting procedure. In some associations, a system of one company, one vote is used. Others use a weighted voting system; then, number of employees, amount of production, or some other variable becomes the measure for determining voting weight.

In extremely large associations, a second questionnaire may be submitted to all members of the association late in the course of collective bargaining. This questionnaire indicates the points of disagreement remaining between the association and the union. Each firm is asked to note in a secret ballot whether it wishes to accede to the union's proposals, to insist on employer proposals, to drop the issue, or to take a strike. In addition, each firm is asked to specify the maximum size of the economic package it is willing to have offered before taking a strike.

A decision on whether to settle for the union's minimum terms or to accept strike action is more complicated within an association than it is in single-firm bargaining. The issue can be resolved, of course, on the basis of a majority vote among employers. The professional staff, however, usually evaluates the solidarity of the employer group in the face of a possible strike. If an association takes a strike only to find that some of its members capitulate to the union after a short time, the association is seriously weakened, if not totally destroyed, as a future counterweight to union bargaining power. Many association representatives state that if it appears to them that their employers will not unanimously withstand a strike for an extended period of time, they will do their utmost to encourage the employers to make any settlement necessary in order to avoid a strike situation.

Chapter 8

Joint Union-Management Preparation

MANY management and labor officials have been impressed with the need to break out of time-worn bargaining procedures, and within the past several years numerous attempts to do so have been made. Through continuous consultation arrangements, joint bargaining preparations, and cooperative research efforts, the bargaining parties have attempted to resolve problems free from the tense atmosphere of the bargaining table, where decision-making occurs under the pressure of a strike deadline.

Experience with these new approaches is still too brief to support any judgments about whether they will or will not become firmly embedded industrial relations practices. Several of the experiments have already fallen by the wayside, and others undoubtedly will, also. Some positive results can be noted, however, and if the new arrangements survive and spread they may well be the most significant bargaining innovations of the contemporary period.

The following sections describe in brief detail some of

the more prominent examples of this new process of joint preparation and continuous consultation. In several of the situations, the parties have worked with third-party neutrals. In others, the approach has remained bipartite in character.

Examples of Joint Study and Preparation

One of the earliest endeavors in joint preparation was that undertaken by the Armour Company and two of the principal unions with which it deals—the United Packinghouse Workers of America and the Amalgamated Meat Cutters and Butcher Workmen of North America.[1] The parties agreed that a fund of $500,000, raised through company payments of 1 cent per cwt of total tonnage shipped from certain meatpacking plants, was to finance the work of an Automation Committee. Members of the committee included representatives of the company, the two unions, and an impartial chairman.

The committee's function was to study the problems growing out of automation and to make recommendations to the parties. Neutral public members were also engaged to undertake background studies for the information of the committee. Confidential recommendations were made to the parties by the impartial chairman prior to their 1961 negotiations. Initial projects recommended by the committee, which involved the relocation and re-

---

[1] Detailed discussions of the Armour Committee's work may be found in Thomas Kennedy, *Automation Funds and Displaced Workers* (Harvard University Graduate School of Business Administration, 1962), pp. 129–60; and Frederick R. Livingston, "An Approach to Automation," *Proceedings, New York University 14th Annual Conference on Labor,* 1961, pp. 301–11.

training of workers, were not overly successful. Some later projects have given more reason for optimism.

In very brief summary, during the two or three years following the committee's establishment its work had beneficial effects on the bargaining relationship between the Armour Company and the two unions involved. The relationship became more stable, wildcat strikes diminished, and the parties came part of the way, at least, toward a solution of their mutual problems.

Another significant example of joint study and preparation undertaken to resolve labor–management difficulties is one on the West Coast, involving the Pacific Maritime Association and the International Longshoremen's and Warehousemen's Union.[2] The West Coast longshore industrial relationship had, for many years, been characterized by intermittent union warfare against mechanization and by union insistence on restrictive work rules to guarantee employment.

After two years of informal discussions, an interim agreement between the parties was arranged in 1959. This agreement was in force during the collection and development of data whereby union members were to receive some sort of concrete financial benefits in return for giving the employer freedom to adopt new laborsaving methods as well as for dropping certain restrictive working rules.

From 1959 through October, 1960, the parties engaged in extended discussions and negotiations that led to a

---

[2] Details of this undertaking may be found in Kennedy, *op. cit.*, pp. 70–101; Lincoln Fairley, "The ILWU-PMA Mechanization and Modernization Agreement," *Labor Law Journal*, July, 1961; and Charles C. Killingsworth, "The Modernization of West Coast Longshore Work Rules," *Industrial and Labor Relations Review*, April, 1962.

final agreement under which the men were given a "share of the machine." An ultimate total of $29 million was to be paid into a fund to be shared among class A registered longshoremen. In return, the employer received freedom to mechanize, and he gained substantial relief from a number of working rules that had restricted productivity improvements.

Two joint committees established in the basic steel industry are also noteworthy in connection with the development of joint preparation and joint continuous problem-solving relationships. The United Steelworkers of America made one such agreement separately with the Kaiser Steel Corporation,[3] and it affected another with most of the largest producers in the basic steel industry. The second agreement also established a Steel Human Relations Committee.[4]

The Kaiser Steel "long-range sharing plan" arose from the separate settlement negotiated between the company and the United Steelworkers of America in 1959. The parties in that settlement agreed to the establishment of a tripartite committee to recommend a long-range plan for sharing the fruits of the company's progress among the stockholders, the employees, and the public.

In late 1962, the parties announced that they had agreed on a plan which, among other things, guaranteed employees substantial protection against the loss of jobs

---

[3] For specific details, see "The Kaiser-Steel Union Sharing Plan," National Industrial Conference Board, 1963; and A. H. Raskin, "Approach to Automation: The Kaiser Plan," *New York Times Magazine,* November 3, 1963.

[4] See R. Heath Larry, "Steel's Human Relations Committee," *Steelways,* September, 1963; and Harry Seligson, "Breakthroughs in Labor–Management Relations," *Labor Law Journal,* June, 1963.

or income because of technological changes introduced by the company. It also assured employees a 32.5 percent share of any cost savings that result from increased efficiencies or from any other source. Under this sharing plan, both employees and the company have received substantial benefits from the savings made. Moreover, the relationships between employees, their union, and the company seem to have been improved as a result of the degree of cooperation shown by the parties.

The steel industry's Human Relations Committee also grew out of the 1959 strike settlement. As a consequence of the strike, the bargaining parties seemed to feel that some new approach was needed in their relationship. The Human Relations Committee became the vehicle through which an attempt was made to develop a new relationship.

The HRC is a bipartite committee of high-level representatives from the industry and the union, but, unlike the Kaiser agreement, it has no third-party membership. The committee, through a number of subcommittees, undertook a series of long-range studies relating to labor-management problems in the steel industry. The committee also served as a forum wherein the parties engaged in full and frank private discussions, with the prior understanding that neither side was to become publicly committed to positions it had argued.

The basic steel industry contract was renegotiated twice without serious difficulty, and the work of the Human Relations Committee was accorded a large share of credit for these smooth settlements. The committee, however, played little or no role in the 1965 negotiations. In light of political developments within the union, the committee's future does not appear to be promising.

In addition to these examples of joint study committees, several less well-publicized but similar committees have been established in other industries. One agreement of this type was reached in 1961 by the United Automobile Workers of America and the American Motors Corporation. Although it was overshadowed by the profit-sharing feature of that agreement, a provision called for a "continuing forum" in which the parties could freely discuss long-range mutual problems. The forum has had some positive results.[5]

Perhaps as a reflection of this agreement, the big three automobile manufacturers in 1963 acceded to a request from the United Automobile Workers that 12-man labor-management committees be established at each company. These committees engaged in joint studies preparatory to the 1964 automobile negotiations.

Both in 1961 and in 1963, several months before their actual negotiations, the General Electric Company and the International Union of Electrical Workers participated in joint study groups concerned with specific anticipated problem areas. Their hope was that by means of such groups they could reach some agreement on particularly knotty problems prior to their actual negotiations.

Similar types of specific problem-oriented joint committees have been established by the major can companies and the steelworkers. The International Ladies Garment Workers' Union and one of the nation's leading dress manufacturers, Bobbie Brooks, Inc., recently established a joint committee for continuing study of wage structures, production standards, and employee welfare. This com-

---

[5] Edward L. Cushman, "The American Motors-United Automobile Workers Progress Sharing Agreement," *Proceedings, 14th Annual Meeting, Industrial Relations Research Association*, 1961.

mittee has engaged a prominent neutral to serve as chairman.

In several industries, joint study committees have been established at the instigation of the government. This was true of the Presidential Railroad Commission, which undertook a 15-month series of studies, looking toward a possible settlement of the working rules dispute between the operating brotherhoods and the railroad carriers. A similar type of government-sponsored study was undertaken in connection with negotiations in the Atlantic and Gulf Coast longshore industry prior to its 1964 negotiations. Neither of these government-sponsored and supported committees was immediately instrumental in resolving the bargaining impasses that led to their creation, though each may well have made a contribution to the long-run resolution of some industry problems.

Trends and Problems in Joint Preparation

The evidence suggests that an increase in the amount of joint preparation and early negotiations is taking place throughout the industrial community. The Federal Mediation and Conciliation Service has noted that the establishment of joint study committees is a significant feature in an ever-increasing number of the negotiated settlements on which it reports.

Numerous unions, including District 50 of the United Mineworkers and some of the District Lodges of the International Association of Machinists, are engaging in concerted efforts to establish such committees wherever possible. Many employer associations are attempting to create joint committees in order to improve the climate of industrial relations in their industries. The National

Electrical Contractors Association and the International Brotherhood of Electrical Workers, for example, have for many years maintained a voluntary Council on Industrial Relations for settling disputes within the industry after deadlocks occur. This council appears, in some situations and in some areas, to be moving toward area-wide mechanisms to avoid disputes.

The American Arbitration Association is sponsoring programs in several industries. During these programs, prominent management and union representatives meet with well-known neutrals in the labor-management field to discuss industrial relations problems of their particular industries.

There appears to be some tendency, moreover, for this approach—joint problem-solving away from the pressures of contract termination dates—to develop without new committees or groups being established specifically for the purpose. In several industry associations, employer-union committees established to administer pension and health and welfare programs are broadening their functions and responsibilities by undertaking discussions about long-range labor-management problems in their industries.

Conclusion

A prominent labor leader has criticized the sort of collective bargaining that is only "a kind of brief encounter every two or three years." The consultative arrangements described in this chapter are efforts to circumvent the disadvantages inherent when the collective bargaining relationship is limited to periods of negotiations. As noted earlier, judgments about the success of the new approaches would be premature. Without the anchors of tradition and usage, they are vulnerable, and any disenchantment on the part of either labor or management is liable to bring a promising experiment to an abrupt halt. This has apparently happened in the case of the steel industry's Human Relations Committee.

It can be anticipated that some of the other experiments will have something less than complete success. The bargaining parties, however, are under strong pressures to modernize the bargaining process. The increasingly technical character of the subjects of bargaining, the special challenge posed by a technological revolution, and the emergence of a public impatience with bargaining failures are among the factors that are pushing labor and management in the direction of more efficient bargaining arrangements.

It is unlikely that the traditional bargaining methods will be able to withstand all these pressures. Thus, the experiments in joint preparations for bargaining can be regarded as first reactions to the cumulative forces that are pushing in the direction of modernized bargaining methods. Regardless of the fate of these pioneer efforts, further innovations can be anticipated.

Chapter 9

Summary and Conclusion

In LARGER FIRMS and in multiemployer organizations, the act of preparing for bargaining has come to be an involved affair. Dozens—sometimes even hundreds—of people participate at one point or another in the preparatory process. These people are drawn not only from the industrial relations staffs but also from many other company departments whose main activities are not concerned with labor relations. This is not a haphazard development but, rather, reflects management personnel's becoming more concerned about the quality of their preparations than they were 15 years ago. As a consequence, the job is now undertaken more systematically in many bargaining situations.

Review of the Study

In the interviews that provided the bulk of the data for this study, the management respondents, without exception, affirmed the importance they place on adequate preparation. Many insisted that there was a close relationship between the quality of management's preparations and the results achieved through the collective bargaining process. It is interesting, however, that despite their consensus concerning the importance of preparation activities management personnel, on the whole, were found to have a rather hazy knowledge of practices in firms other than their own. Moreover, very few thought that their own firms did as good a preparation job as they might. A few management representatives interviewed found it quite difficult to systematically describe their own activities, even though they themselves had been engaged in bargaining preparations for many years.

As noted in the first chapter, the main object of the present study has been to describe collective bargaining preparations in the firms and bargaining associations that participated in the study. Though concerned with activities that, for the most part, take place before bargaining begins, the study nevertheless casts light on the whole of the labor negotiation process.

There is a fairly obvious, but important, relationship between the ways in which management prepares itself for bargaining and the methods by which it actually bargains. While strategy may change in the course of negotiations, initial positions taken by management—positions that reflect the data collected and the decisions reached during the preparation period—fundamentally condition the whole course of labor negotiations.

Findings

The major findings of the study, described in greater detail in earlier chapters, can be summarized as follows.

1. Although responsibility for bargaining preparation is placed differently from firm to firm, generally the industrial relations unit assumes primary responsibility for preparations in the noneconomic area, while other de-

partments bear the responsibility for the wage-fringe package. It is not unusual, however, for staff industrial relations people to exercise some influence in the economic sphere. Furthermore, in the economic area no one class of corporate officers typically exercises more decisional authority than any other.

2. The length of time spent in direct preparation for bargaining tends to vary with the complexity of the bargaining structure. Large multiplant firms usually begin to prepare about nine months before the start of bargaining, while the average time spent by smaller firms is slightly less. Preparation time is shorter—about three to four months—for individual employers who bargain through a professional negotiator associated with an employer bargaining association.

3. Managements generally begin their preparations with an analysis of contract administration problems. The wage package that will be offered is usually not constructed until a relatively late stage of the preparation period. There are various reasons for this timing. Management wants first to evaluate whether it will make proposals for major contract changes that it may have to buy. It wants the latest possible information on other collective bargaining settlements that may influence its own. In some situations, considerations of secrecy dictate the desirability of postponing discussions of management's economic offer. Finally, many companies want to hear the union's whole package of proposals before considering an economic counterproposal.

4. In addition to determining the size of the economic package that will constitute the company offer, final preparations include shaping specific proposals for changes in contract language, preparation of statistical

and visual displays, and compilation of a bargaining book for the use of company negotiators.

5. Preparations undertaken relative to contract administration are made for both offensive and defensive purposes. For the offense category, preparation typically involves a canvass of plant managers and others to uncover particularly disadvantageous contract language, preparation of proposals embodying more suitable language, and consideration of bargaining strategies for accomplishing the desired changes. Activities undertaken in defense of sections in the agreement with which management is satisfied consist basically of efforts to anticipate the union's bargaining goals; then data are collected to illustrate the beneficial impact of existing clauses.

6. The character of preparation for wage bargaining varies considerably among firms. Such preparations may consist of little more than a costing-out of different wage proposals. Or they may be more complex; some may go as far as a detailed economic analysis, designed to support the company position before the public and various government bodies as well as in the negotiating room. Although many firms analyze productivity data and collect cost-of-living information, most of them do not believe that such data figure prominently in the actual bargaining.

7. Most company negotiators believe that a knowledge of the union and of leading personalities within the union is helpful for bargaining purposes. Various kinds of information are collected and recorded to increase the bargaining team's knowledge of personal or political problems that influence the course of negotiations.

8. Intercompany cooperation for collective bargaining occurs in many ways. In addition to the practice of joint

bargaining, companies may cooperate through joint preparations, even though they bargain separately. Less formally, many companies exchange information, and do so at many different levels of their management hierarchies. The extent of such information exchanges among firms that do not otherwise cooperate appears to be very substantial. This may have been suspected heretofore, but little real information on the subject has been accumulated or analysis made of its effects.

9. Although the overall amount is small, there has been, in recent years, some growth in the areas of company-union cooperation for research and joint consultation prior to the start of negotiations. The increasingly technical nature of bargaining, a growing public impatience with bargaining failures, and an awareness on the part of union and management representatives of the deficiencies of traditional bargaining are among the factors that have moved the bargaining parties to search for fresh approaches in their collective relationships.

Conclusion

Although no attempt has been made to relate the findings of this study to recently developed theories of collective bargaining, our data appear to have implications relevant to certain aspects of the bargaining models constructed by theoreticians. Two of these can be noted briefly.

The Unity of Management

It is perhaps misleading to assume that the web of managerial relationships can adequately or accurately be personified by the term "management." Academic analysts of collective bargaining are quite aware that many points of view are represented by different sections or different individuals in a company's organizational hierarchy, but it is usually assumed that these crystallize, at some point of time, into a single, unified management position. In some situations, the assumption is a reasonable approximation of reality. In others, however, it leads to a distorted picture of the bargaining process.

A recent perceptive study of one aspect of the labor–management relationship highlights the point. Margaret Chandler has noted that when issues arise within a firm concerning the contracting out of work certain sections of management typically line up with the inside union, while others array themselves with the outside union.[1] Our interviews similarly elicited many examples of several "management" positions that existed simultaneously during the preparation process. Frequently, what we found was not a convergence of opposing viewpoints into a single management preference but, rather, a situation in which one viewpoint became dominant over another.

The difficulties faced by the industrial relations departments in many organizations bear witness to the argument made here. Industrial relations personnel, who will be intimately involved in the administration of any agreement reached in bargaining, are sensitive about the workability of the final bargaining outcome. Industrial relations, thus, will frequently oppose a bargaining position that is vindictive, ideologically oriented, or simply naïve.

Other elements in management, however, may react against a counsel of moderation and regard industrial

---

[1] Margaret K. Chandler, *Management Rights and Union Interests* (New York: McGraw-Hill Book Co., Inc., 1964).

relations as being insufficiently aggressive. In one of the firms interviewed, an industrial relations director had lost his job because operating plant managers felt that a particular bargaining concession had been too generous. His plea that the decision was made in the course of multi-employer bargaining and, thus, beyond his control was to no avail.

In essence, the nub of the professional labor relations man's problem is the largely unreal stereotype of his role held by most of the public and many of his management colleagues, who see him locked in unremitting conflict with the union representatives with whom he bargains. The view is epitomized by an often-heard complaint within the fraternity: "I'm having more trouble with my company than I am with the union."

As industrial and labor relations have become professionalized—i.e., increasingly conducted by men educated and trained for this specific work—a certain mutuality of interest has grown up between them and their union counterparts. Each believes in the right of the other to exist and to defend certain objectives, and each understands and lives by a number of commonly accepted rules of the game. Yet, these beliefs often are not fully or strongly shared by the remainder of the management group. Their attitudes are entirely understandable, since their functional roles depend little, if at all, on maintaining viable relationships with union representatives. The job-related values and priorities of other management people are usually substantially different than those of labor relations men.

In these circumstances, to speak of the development of a consensus "management" position in regard to a forthcoming negotiation is often illusory. Management is multifaced and multivoiced, and its position is simply the one most strongly defended at any given point in time. Furthermore, a shift from the position of one group to that of another occurs only as more "desirable" positions become untenable in the face of union pressure. Analysis of management decision-making in the process of preparing to bargain should often, therefore, be based upon a pluralistic, rather than a unitary, management model. Management preparation for bargaining in many of the companies interviewed during this study is less a search for consensus than it is a shifting of priorities and preferences among previously existing and oftentimes competing "management positions."

Preparation and the Search for Agreement

Another point frequently made by students of the bargaining process is supported by the present study. Some theories of bargaining describe the process as one in which the parties attempt to determine ranges of compatibility within their respective positions. To the extent that uncertainties about the true position of one's opponent in bargaining can be removed, the process of finding areas of overlap or agreement is simplified.

Our analysis indicates that a substantial part of the preparation undertaken is designed to lessen the amount of uncertainty in collective bargaining. If removal of uncertainty is the first step toward agreement, then preparation for bargaining should properly be viewed as part and parcel of the search for agreement, not as something preceding it. For example, much of the financial data collected is used for the purpose of quantifying and thus removing uncertainty about the possible costs of bargaining outcomes. In theoretical terminology, it is an attempt to transform management utility functions into monetary terms.

Preparations described in Chapter 6 are essentially for the purpose of reducing the range of uncertainty about union reaction to management proposals. Analysis of union constitutions, union publications, and statements of union officers is undertaken in the hope that the nego- tiator's predictive capacities will be enhanced.

One of the most interesting developments in the con- temporary collective bargaining experience is the ten- dency for both labor and management to minimize un- certainty by a direct exchange of information. In what is called traditional, or distributive, bargaining, the par- ties use bargaining skill to differentiate serious from rela- tively frivolous items in the proposals of the opposite side. Now, in informal prebargaining meetings it is not un- usual for management and labor negotiators to inform each other about proposals that each regards as especially important.

This informational exchange is an important element of what has been called the "attitudinal structuring" model.[2] In situations of this type, it becomes less and less possible to distinguish between bargaining preparations and bargaining itself. The search for agreement, begin- ning at the preparation stage, becomes an extended and continuous process.

The type of exchange described here is not typical. However, the degree of labor-management decision-mak- ing that presently occurs outside formal bargaining ses-

---

[2] Richard E. Walton and Robert B. McKersie, *A Behavioral Theory of Labor Negotiations* (New York: McGraw-Hill Book Co., Inc., 1965).

sions supports—tentatively, at least—the long-run possibility of a substantial decline or even complete atrophy of adversary negotiations over the bargaining table.

Talks between labor and management over terms of new contracts will continue inevitably, but their nature and environment may change substantially. The arrangements for continuous consultations, joint labor-management research, and joint preparation activities, as well as the informal consultations described in earlier chapters, may appear to be of slight significance in the overall picture of American collective bargaining. They may be harbingers of things to come, however.

Collective bargaining, whatever its merits, has a number of deficiencies as a means of arriving at decisions. There is at least the possibility that the changes in bargaining methods that have already occurred will be followed by yet further developments of like character.

A Brief Description of the Bargaining Process

IN A BROAD SENSE, collective bargaining can be described as a method of making decisions. Through selected representatives, workers bargain with employers over the terms and conditions of employment. When workers are unorganized, decisional authority in these matters rests with the employer, although his degree of discretion is subject to a variety of economic, legal, and social constraints. The basic nature of collective bargaining can be described simply, but the subject itself is complex because the forms, subject matter, and processes of bargaining vary significantly among situations. Consequently, general statements about these matters must be carefully qualified.

Organization for Bargaining Purposes

The bargaining process is conditioned, of course, by the ways in which the parties organize themselves for bargaining purposes. On the union side, bargaining units are usually described as either craft or industrial units. In craft units, membership consists of persons who make up

141

a homogeneous occupational group such as carpenters, printers, or bricklayers. In industrial units, workers are organized on the basis of the product produced. Thus, an industrial unit of auto workers may include highly skilled tool and die makers, semiskilled assemblers, and unskilled material handlers. In practice, many units do not conform completely to the pure craft or industrial type, but it is usually possible to classify employee units as craftlike or industrial-like on the basis of their more prominent characteristics.

An employer may bargain individually, or he may join with fellow employers in his industry for bargaining purposes. The single employer may bargain separately with groups of employees such as electricians, truck drivers, and production workers, or he may bargain with all the employees grouped together in a comprehensive industrial unit. When the employing firm is a multiplant operation, the possible bargaining arrangements multiply in number. An employer with several plants, for instance, may negotiate separately for each plant or with a union unit that represents employees in two or more plants. The most comprehensive unit possible as long as the employer bargains individually is a company-wide unit.

Although individual employer bargaining is the most common arrangement, multiemployer bargaining is not uncommon. About one third of all employees under contract are covered by agreements reached between unions and associations of employers. Multiemployer groupings may be local, regional, or industry-wide.

In many fairly large industries, all employers who have labor contracts with locals of the same international union join to bargain with a single union committee that represents all the locals involved. This type of arrangement occurs in basic steel, hard and soft coal, and among longshore employers within given coastal areas.

Groups of employers in an industry may also join to bargain simultaneously with a committee composed of representatives of different unions. For example, the railroad carriers have negotiated simultaneously with five unions of railroad operating employees, or as many as eleven different unions representing various nonoperating crafts. Similarly, shipping employer associations often negotiate simultaneously with several unions of licensed or unlicensed seafarers.

Finally, multiemployer groups are often formed to negotiate with a single local union that represents employees at each of the firms. This sort of organization is becoming increasingly common within metropolitan areas, particularly where many small employers face a single powerful union. Examples occur in local cartage agreements with the International Brotherhood of Teamsters, when retailers negotiate with a city-wide local of the Retail Clerks International Association, or when small dress manufacturers in one area join to bargain with the International Ladies Garment Workers' Union. Employer associations for joint local bargaining have often been deliberately fostered and encouraged by the unions involved.

Employer bargaining groups vary widely in type, structure, procedure, and scope of activity. Some substantial employer groups have established formal membership associations, frequently incorporated as nonprofit organizations under state law. Others simply act through joint bargaining committees, without incorporation. Still others employ a single negotiator and authorize him, by power of attorney, to conduct their bargaining. Whatever the arrangement, multiemployer bargaining is essentially consensual, having its roots in the parties' voluntary acceptance of this method of bargaining.

The above description of bargaining structures, while skeletal, is sufficient to suggest the rich variety found in the American collective bargaining experience. The sources of bargaining complexity, however, are not limited to these structural forms. The exact quality of a particular bargaining process may reflect such varied factors as economic condition of the firm, personalities and ideologies of the company and union officers, past history of industrial relations in a particular industry, and styles of negotiation.

In large corporate and union organizations, furthermore, it is unlikely that personnel at all levels and in all specializations will hold common views as to appropriate bargaining goals or methods of achieving such goals. In labor organizations, for example, general internal conflict as well as conflict specific to the bargaining process may be generated by different evaluations of bargaining targets at national and local union headquarters, by divergence of interests between skilled and unskilled workers, or by internal union politics. Within corporations, personnel in departments such as sales, production, and finance may hold quite different ideas about the ways in which corporate interests would be best served in labor negotiations.

In brief, then, the widely held view of collective bargaining as a type of contest between labor and management, though not incorrect, is simplistic. An understanding of the dynamics of the bargaining process requires some appreciation of the complexities that flow from bargaining structures, the social and economic constraints that bear on the negotiators, and the internal characteristics of union and company organizations.

Characteristics of the Collective Bargaining Relationship

Students of collective bargaining have advanced a number of general explanations of what is involved in collective bargaining. Under the marketing theory, collective bargaining is considered to be primarily a means of establishing the price of labor. This explanation follows a popular conception of labor-management negotiations. In its original and primitive form in the United States, collective bargaining was, essentially, a method of marketing labor. Workers posted lists of rates at which they would work, and employers could elect to either accept the rates or contest them. If employers contested, the matter was settled through a test of strength between workers and employers.

As collective bargaining grew in complexity, it became obvious that important features of bargaining were unexplained by a marketing theory. Two explanations that attempt to deal with certain complexities are the governmental theory and managerial theory.

The governmental theory suggests that collective bargaining is a form of industrial government. The basic labor–management contract is described as being analogous to a constitution. Management, charged with the duty of carrying out the contract, is likened to the executive branch of government. The negotiating committees, which amend or elaborate the contract, constitute the legislative branch. The grievance procedure, through which executive actions are challenged, is the judicial branch. This explanation directs attention to the fact that the bargaining relationship is a continuing one and that sovereignty in the workplace is shared by management and worker representatives.

Under the managerial theory, collective bargaining is described as a method or procedure for making business decisions. Since decisions about wages and working conditions *are* management decisions, labor as well as management personnel is engaged in the process of management. This theory, then, visualizes collective bargaining as a sharing of management. It emphasizes that when collective bargaining is accepted as a decision-making procedure a basic change in the management institution occurs, and that final directive authority as well as limited administrative authority is exercised by both labor and management in certain decision-making spheres of the business firm.

The marketing theory concentrates on the wage decision and, thus, has an economic orientation. The governmental theory tries to explain the political character of the bargaining process, and the managerial theory focuses on the decision-making process in the firm and asserts that authority is shared by labor and management in certain areas. The three approaches are not inconsistent. In fact, they supplement one another and, taken together, provide a comprehensive picture of the broad character of the bargaining process.

The Bargaining Conference

The same heterogeneity that characterizes other aspects of the American labor–management relationship is found in the actual act of bargaining. A union may be represented at the conference table by an individual or a committee. When bargaining is done through a committee, the negotiators may be union officers or they may be representatives selected directly by the rank and file.

Ordinarily, union officers predominate in a negotiating committee. When negotiations are conducted nationally, the bargaining committee usually consists of national union officials reinforced, perhaps, by members of the executive board and selected local officials.

On the management side, bargaining may be done by a line officer, such as a vice-president in charge of production, or by a staff officer, such as the industrial relations director. Other possible negotiators are company attorneys, bargaining attorneys retained especially for the task, bargaining experts supplied by employer associations, or committees drawn from the membership of a trade association. In smaller firms, bargaining is occasionally done by the proprietor or the corporate president.

Each side may be represented by large numbers of persons or by relatively small groups. Even when many people are present, actual negotiations will usually be conducted by one or a few representatives of each side.

What goes on at the bargaining conference? Here, too, we find a good deal of variation from situation to situation. In some relationships, especially when the balance of power is heavily weighted in favor of one side, bargaining may consist of little more than a unilateral imposition of terms by the more powerful bargaining party. This type of situation has been aptly described as "collective bludgeoning." In other relationships, bargaining consists of a give-and-take type of trading, not totally unlike what goes on in marketplace haggling over a commodity price.

In many situations, however, the parties enter into negotiations with predetermined positions or, at least, with strong preferences for certain positions within a range of possible bargaining outcomes. Bargaining, here, becomes less a matter of trading than an effort to determine the opposite party's true settlement position and an attempt to deploy bargaining power to move the settlement position in a favorable direction if it lies outside a party's idea of the minimum it can accept. If the move is not possible, power is exerted, usually in the form of a threatened strike or stated willingness to accept a work stoppage, in order to convince the bargaining partner that it would be less costly to modify his settlement position than to rigidly hold to it.

In actual practice, the normal outcome of the bargaining process is a peaceful settlement of differences and a mutually agreeable solution. Over 100,000 labor agreements are consummated each year in the United States, and work stoppages occur in only a small percentage of all negotiations. The possibility of economic harm that each party can exert on the other serves as the mutual prod to keep them at the bargaining table, seeking areas of compromise and accommodation.

The facts obtained and the materials gathered during the preparation stage are far from extraneous to the power relationships involved in the bargaining process, however. They serve a threefold purpose: they are essential to each negotiator in determining his own position in bargaining; they serve to aid him as he seeks from others in his organization an understanding of the positions he takes and the compromises he offers; and they also serve, in some part, to convince the other party of the reasonableness of his position.

Index

149

MANAGEMENT PREPARATION FOR COLLECTIVE BARGAINING

By

Meyer S. Ryder, LL.B.

Graduate School of Business Administration, University of Michigan; former Public Member of the Wage Stabilization Board; served as Regional Director of the National Labor Relations Board in Cleveland, Ohio and Buffalo, New York; member, Board of Governors of the National Academy of Arbitrators.

Charles M. Rehmus, Ph.D.

Former Commissioner, Federal Mediation and Conciliation Service, and Labor Relations Advisor, Secretary of Commerce. Presently with Institute of Labor and Industrial Relations, University of Michigan-Wayne State University.

Sanford Cohen, Ph.D.

Department of Economics, University of New Mexico. Former—Examiner, National Labor Relations Board; Branch Chief, Wage Stabilization Board. Faculty Director, U. S. Department of Labor, International Manpower Institute, Summer 1966.